DEFERRED GLORY

HEROES OF THE NEGRO BASEBALL LEAGUES

DANNY A. INGELLIS

Deferred Glory

Copyright © 2021 by Danny A. Ingellis

All rights reserved

Published by Red Penguin Books

Bellerose Village, New York

Library of Congress Control Number: 2021900911

ISBN

Print 978-1-63777-015-3 / 978-1-63777-025-2

Digital 978-1-63777-016-0

No part of this book may be reproduced in any form or by any electronic or mechanical means, including information storage and retrieval systems, without written permission from the author, except for the use of brief quotations in a book review.

PRAISE FOR DANNY A. INGELLIS

It took the Baseball Hall of Fame decades – and not a little prodding – to do right by some of the greatest and best-loved stars of the Negro Leagues.

It took Danny Ingellis six months, as an homage to a friend.

Buck O'Neil would be proud.

— JAY PRICE, RETIRED SPORTSWRITER, AUTHOR OF *THANKSGIVING 1959*

Deferred Glory: Heroes of the Negro Baseball Leagues is a home run! Travel back in time as author Dan Ingellis takes a close-up look of some of the men who played in the Negro Leagues, which provided talented athletes of color a place to play since they were not allowed to participate in the all-white Major Leagues until Jackie Robinson suited up for the Brooklyn Dodgers in 1947. Ingellis details the rampant racism and terrible living conditions the players had to endure. Deferred Glory is a terrific read for any avid baseball fan.

— JOSEPH D'AMODIO, SPORTS JOURNALIST FOR THE STATEN ISLAND ADVANCE & SILIVE.COM

As America moves through another step in its tortured race history, no debut book could be more timely than Dan Ingellis's, "Deferred Glory: Heroes of the Negro Baseball Leagues." The lively collection of brief histories of some of the Negro League stars robbed by our National Pastime's original sin of segregation is a primer on why the lives of men like Monte Irvin should be taught in Middle School classes across the land.

— CORMAC GORDON, BASEBALL HALL OF FAME VOTER AND FORMER NYC NEWSPAPER COLUMNIST

Now that Major League Baseball has recognized the Negro Leagues as major leagues, and is endeavoring to import the statistics of the many players who toiled there for decades, "Deferred Glory: Heroes of the Negro Baseball Leagues" is a timely and fresh look at the stories of the players who excelled in the Negro leagues. Readers will be introduced to those trailblazers who paved the way for so many that followed. Their abilities, personalities, perseverance, and love of the game, are reflected in this easy to read summary which will be appreciated by every baseball fan.

— MARIO MATTEI, SABR MEMBER—SOCIETY FOR AMERICAN BASEBALL RESEARCH

CONTENTS

Foreword	vii
Preface	xi
Prologue	1
1. DEFERRED GLORY	3
2. SATCHEL PAIGE	7
3. JOSH GIBSON	11
4. BUCK LEONARD	17
5. MONTE IRVIN	21
6. COOL PAPA BELL	29
7. WILLIAM "JUDY" JOHNSON	33
8. OSCAR CHARLESTON	37
9. MARTIN DIHIGO	41
10. POP LLOYD	45
11. RUBE FOSTER	49
12. RAY DANDRIDGE	53
13. LEON DAY	57
14. BILL FOSTER	63
15. WILLIE WELLS	67
16. "BULLET" JOE ROGAN	71
17. SMOKEY JOE WILLIAMS	75
18. TURKEY STEARNES	79
19. HILTON SMITH	83
20. RAY BROWN	89
21. WILLARD BROWN	93
22. ANDY COOPER	97
23. FRANK GRANT	101
24. PETE HILL	105
25. BIZ MACKEY	109
26. EFFA MANLEY	113
27. JOSE MENDEZ	119
28. ALEX POMPEZ	123
29. CUMBERLAND POSEY	127
30. LOUIS SANTOP	131

31.	MULE SUTTLES	135
32.	BEN TAYLOR	141
33.	CRISTOBAL TORRIENTE	145
34.	SOLOMON WHITE	151
35.	J. LESLIE WILKINSON	157
36.	JUD WILSON	161
37.	JOHN WESLEY DONALDSON	167
38.	BUCK O'NEIL	173
39.	ROD CAREW	179
40.	MILITARY HEROES OF THE NEGRO LEAGUES	185
41.	PHOTO GALLERY	189
	Acknowledgments	215
	About the Author	217

FOREWORD

This book, which was a long time coming, is about Hall of Fame baseball players, some of the best there ever were, who in some cases never got to show it on the big stage, or had to wait too long to be recognized for it, because of the color of their skin; and because each one of them spent his baseball career, or the best part of it, in the Negro Leagues.

But it started as a favor to a friend, one baseball guy doing a solid for another, something Danny Ingellis knows a little something about.

Ingellis, who spent most of his working life as a New York City cop, grew up a Yankee fan in the projects—the Amsterdam Projects in Manhattan's Hell's Kitchen. He learned to play ball in the street, and in what they used to call the Puerto Rican league in Central Park. When he was still a teenager, Ingellis had a week-long tryout with the big club, up in the Bronx, and not so many years later, after a tour in Vietnam, he played for the Third Army baseball team, representing General George Patton's old outfit.

Andy Mele grew up in Brooklyn, rooting for the Dodgers like all those other guys from Brooklyn, and playing ball with and against the Torre Brothers, Joe and Frank, and Sandy Koufax and Joe Pepitone and a thousand more at the Parade Ground, where 13 diamonds whirred with action from morning to night on the weekend. Long after he retired from working security at the Brooklyn Public Library, as his 70's bled into his 80's, Mele was still playing ball once a week with a group who called themselves the Old Boys of Summer.

So maybe it was inevitable that they'd wind up friends, the Yankee fan and the Dodger fan.

After all those years at the library, surrounded by books, Mele wound up becoming a writer. Mostly, he wrote about what he knew. Baseball. Italians. Italians who played baseball. The old Dodgers. A half-dozen books grew out of those themes, and a series of nostalgia columns in the *Staten Island Advance*.

Ingellis, meantime, became a photographer. He was particularly drawn to flags and sunsets. He sold some of the images, and some he gave away; and over time, some of them found their way into his friend's books and newspaper columns.

When Andy Mele died in the summer of 2020, the two old baseball guys were working on the stories of Julie Bowers, Sonny Logan, and Glenn Mosley, residents of Sandy Ground, one of the country's oldest communities founded by freed Blacks, who played in the last years of the Negro Leagues.

As had become his habit, Ingellis was helping to provide the art; and in their research, both men were surprised to find that nobody had ever done a book commemorating the 35 Negro League giants in baseball's Hall of Fame.

But it wasn't his photographs, or his baseball acumen, that most of his neighbors thought of when they thought of Danny Ingellis.

Years earlier, when he was a driver and bodyguard for the Staten Island district attorney, his boss got sick. Bill Murphy's kidneys were shutting down, and one transplant had already failed. To avoid a dark future attached to a dialysis machine, the D.A. needed a new kidney.

So Ingellis gave him one of his, raising the bar for friendship in that corner of the city.

It was no surprise, then, to the people who know him, that when Andy Mele died with the Negro League projects still unfinished, Ingellis dedicated himself to seeing that the stories of the three Sandy Ground ballplayers made their way into print - and to bringing the tales of the Negro League Hall of Famers together in a book.

Even in normal times, putting a book together and seeing it into print can be daunting for the most experienced author— never mind for a rookie who'd never written anything longer than an arrest report, who was doing it out of a sense of obligation, in the midst of a pandemic.

Just not quite so daunting, perhaps, for a guy who once gave a kidney to a friend.

PREFACE

Almost immediately, from the moment my friend, John Iasparro, introduced me to Andy Mele, I knew we were going to be great and lasting friends. Speaking with Andy that first day, he told me he was a sports fanatic who rooted for the old Brooklyn Dodgers. I told him I too was a sports nut, rooting for the Yankees since the 1950's. Yes, as all fans did from way back, Andy and I were no different, we argued who was a better centerfielder, Duke Snyder or Mickey Mantle. We cheerfully agreed, both were great.

Andy mentioned he had authored a few sports books, one entitled *The Boys of Brooklyn*. I then told Andy I was a photographer, and he told me, "Gee, I could use you on a book I am thinking of writing." I agreed to help Andy. He authored *Caesars of the Diamond*, about Major League players who had Italian last names, as well as players without Italian last names, who were also Italian. Some of my photographs appear in this book, namely, a photo I took of Joe Pepitone when he visited Staten Island Yankee Stadium. The other photo was of the American and Italian flags (which appears on the cover of the book) in front of the Garibaldi Museum on Staten Island. Another book Andy authored which includes my photos is *The*

Italian Squad, about a squad in the NYPD that investigated the Black Hand (prior to the Mafia). Andy's grandfather was part of this original squad, commanded by the legendary, Lt. Joseph Petrosino.

After our first meeting, Andy and I would speak on the phone at least twice a week, mostly about his next book and about the Brooklyn Dodgers and New York Yankees. Our conversation always came to discussing our families—Andy speaking of his two beautiful children, Christine and Andrew, and the love of his life, his granddaughter, Alexandra. My wife and I previously met them at Andy's eightieth birthday party. He was right, they are all beautiful in every way.

Andy would always ask about my wife, Marie, and my daughters, but he was interested in finding out how my grandson Jack was doing in Little League baseball. I would tell Andy, "He's doing great. He hit a ball to left field a "country mile," which he did, off the left field fence for a double." Andy would laugh, saying, "Great!" He then wanted to know how Dakota was doing in gymnastics, and if she won any more medals. I told him, "Andy, she just placed first in Parallel Bars. This was how all our conversations would go, two old guys bragging about their grandchildren.

In March of this year, while speaking with Andy, (just prior to the outbreak of Covid-19) he asked me if I would help him do research on three guys from Staten Island who played baseball in the Negro Leagues. Without hesitation, I agreed. Andy went on to mention the three guys, two of whom I knew. They were Sonny Logan, Glen Mosley and Julie Bowers.

Being a Committeeman on the Staten Island Sports Hall of Fame, I previously met Sonny Logan and Glenn Mosley when they were both Inductees into the Hall. I also met Sonny Logan when he worked at Wagner College. I never met Julie Bowers.

Andy then indicated to me, after I completed my research on these three, that he wanted me to research the Negro players who were inducted into the Baseball Hall of Fame, I again agreed.

In the weeks to come, I'd wind up reading nine books on the Negro Leagues, including one book, *Shades of Glory*, by Lawrence D. Hogan, which was a great book on the players in the Negro Leagues.

In doing my research, it didn't take long to find out all three of the Staten Island ballplayers, now deceased, played for the New York Black Yankees in the final years of the Negro Leagues, from 1947 to 1950, before Bowers and Logan went on to injury-shortened minor-league careers in the Boston and Milwaukee Braves organizations. All three of these players sharpened their skills playing baseball in their youth at Rheinhart Field, located in the Sandy Ground section of Staten Island. Ironically, they all played baseball for Tottenville High School on Staten Island, prior to joining the New York Black Yankees.

I phoned Andy two weeks later and informed him I completed doing the research on Logan, Bowers and Mosley and would drop the paperwork off at his house. It was then he told me he was going into the hospital in the morning just for a checkup. Andy remained in the hospital overnight. I eventually dropped off the paperwork, placing it in his mailbox, as he and I agreed that it wasn't good to make contact because of Covid-19.

No more than two days later, I received a phone call from Andy's daughter Christine, informing me Andy went back to the hospital as he wasn't feeling any better. I briefly spoke with Andy; I could tell by his voice he was not doing good.

We spoke about the article on Bowers, Logan and Mosley, but I could tell Andy was not his old self. I told him I would speak to him the next day.

The next day was August 8th. I received a phone call from Christine informing me Andy had passed away in the hospital. Needless to say, I was saddened to no end. I attended Andy's wake and Funeral Mass. I surely miss him even to this day.

In closing, I say, "Andy, this book's for you."

PROLOGUE

I thought I knew. But I did not.

To create this book, I had to dig deep to find the individual stories of these talented athletes. And my research brought me face-to-face with the hardships these men endured as they pursued their dreams of the Major Leagues.

What started as a simple compilation became so much more complex. I began to understand them at a much deeper level through my excavation of their lives, and as I learned about all their daily indignities—how they had to deal with discrimination in the South *and* the North, on the ballfield *and* on the battlefield—it was as if I was having a private conversation with each one of them in which they shared their innermost thoughts.

. . .

Now I know—and every single one of them has my respect. Despite the odds and ever-present obstacles, these strong-willed men lived proudly, with honor and distinction.

And now you will know, too, as you read these stories of hope, spirit, and survival that combine to light the way to a better tomorrow.

1

DEFERRED GLORY

When I decided to author this book about the black baseball players in the Negro Leagues, I researched the Negro Leagues and its players, reading about nine books, including Lawrence D. Hogan's *Shades of Glory*.

I was amazed and saddened to learn how these players were treated by their owners and the public when they traveled to play their games.

Racism was rampant in the South, as the Jim Crow Laws were in effect, prohibiting blacks from integrating with the white population. These players traveled many miles to play games. Their transportation was on rickety old buses or cars. They were denied occupancy in hotels owned by white proprietors. Some hotels would accept them as they had signs reading BLACKS ONLY. These hotels were roach infested, toilets that would overflow and lacked running water.

. . .

Because of this, the players chose to sleep in the stands inside the ballparks where they would play their games. Others slept on the rickety buses they traveled in. Most of these teams would play three games in one day in order to make ends meet. They would play a game in one city then traveled to another town far away for the next game. Just imagine, they were subjected to these conditions and yet remained determined to play baseball. They did this for practically no wages or very little wages.

These players, in order to make money, would sell programs at the games where they were to play. Fans who sat in the bleachers were charged 25 cents per program, those sitting in the grandstands were charged 50 cents and the fans sitting in field level seats were charged $1. Those who refused to buy a program were escorted from the stadium. The money collected from the sale of these programs was divided up between the teams. This was to be the salary for the game. Some games only drew 500 to 1,000 fans.

The Jim Crow Laws in the South prevented these players from playing games against white teams, or white teams refused to play against black teams.

One area where the Jim Crow Laws were not in effect was in matters of the Federal Government. Some of these black ballplayers were drafted into military service during World War II or some even joined in order to make more money. Whatever their reason, they served proudly and with distinction. After World War II, no black person was awarded the Medal of Honor, but in 1997, President Bill Clinton upgraded those who received the Distinguished Service Cross to the Medal of Honor. Eight families were given the Medal of Honor for their loved ones who were now deceased, but one Medal of Honor was awarded to a living recipient.

THE COLORED LEAGUE

All the Preliminaries Arranged for a Colored Base Ball Association.

The National League of Colored Base Ball Players held their first convention at Eurka Hall on Arthur street, Pittsburg, Dec. 9. The representatives present selected Nelson M. Williams, of Washington, as temporary chairman, and J. Will Gatewood as secretary. The following teams were represented: Philadelphia, by Gilbert A. Ball and R.G. Still; Baltimore, by J.J. Callis; Washington , by Nelson M. Williams; Cincinnati, by J.W. Fowler; Louisville, by L. Condon; Pittsburgh, by Walter S. Brown. The following permanent officers were then chosen: President, Walter S. Brown, of Pittsburg; vice president, J.J. Callis, of Baltimore; secretary, N.M. Williams, of Washington; treasurer, Gilbert A. Ball, of Philadelphia; assistant secretary, M.A. Spriggs, of Pittsburg; board of directors, Horace McGee, J.J. Callis, L. Condon and R. G. Still; schedule committee, W.S. Brown, M.A. Spriggs, Horace McGee, L. Condon and R.G. Still; committee on constitution, J.J. Callis, J.W. Fowler, N.M. Williams and R.G. Still. Upon taking his office President Brown welcomed the delegates in a neat address of welcome. The Spalding ball was adopted. On the question of the adoption of the National rules for 1887, as passed by the League and the Association committees, there was a lively debate, but the motion adopting them was carried. The convention adjourned to meet in March, at the call of President Brown. Boston and Cleveland both sent letters guaranteeing their acceptance of places in the League, and the teams were accordingly enrolled. The meeting was enthusiastic.

Sporting Life, December 15, 1886

The Colored League Poster

After researching the Negro League and how these

black players were treated, I came away with the thought that these men had the burning desire to become ballplayers and possibly make it into the Major Leagues, and therefore withstood the racial abuse and low wages in the hope their dream would come true.

Integration finally broke through in the Major Leagues in 1947 with the signing of Jackie Robinson to a minor league contract. But many black ballplayers who played in the Negro League were deceased by then or too old to realize their dream.

2

SATCHEL PAIGE

BORN: LEROY ROBERT PAGE on July 7, 1906 at
  Mobile, Alabama
DIED: June 8, 1982 at Kansas City, Missouri
Inducted into the National Baseball Hall of Fame
  in 1971

Satchel Paige was the First Negro League player inducted into the Baseball Hall of Fame.

Satchel once explained, "Our last name was changed from Page to Paige, as my parents placed in "i" to make themselves sound more high-toned." Ironically, Satchel learned the skills that made him an accomplished baseball player while in reform school. At the age of 12 years old, while in reform school, Edward Byrd, the school's baseball coach, took young Satchel under his wing and taught him the fundamentals of the game. For the first time, Satchel listened. Satchel admitted, "It was Coach Byrd who taught me how to play baseball and how to be disciplined."

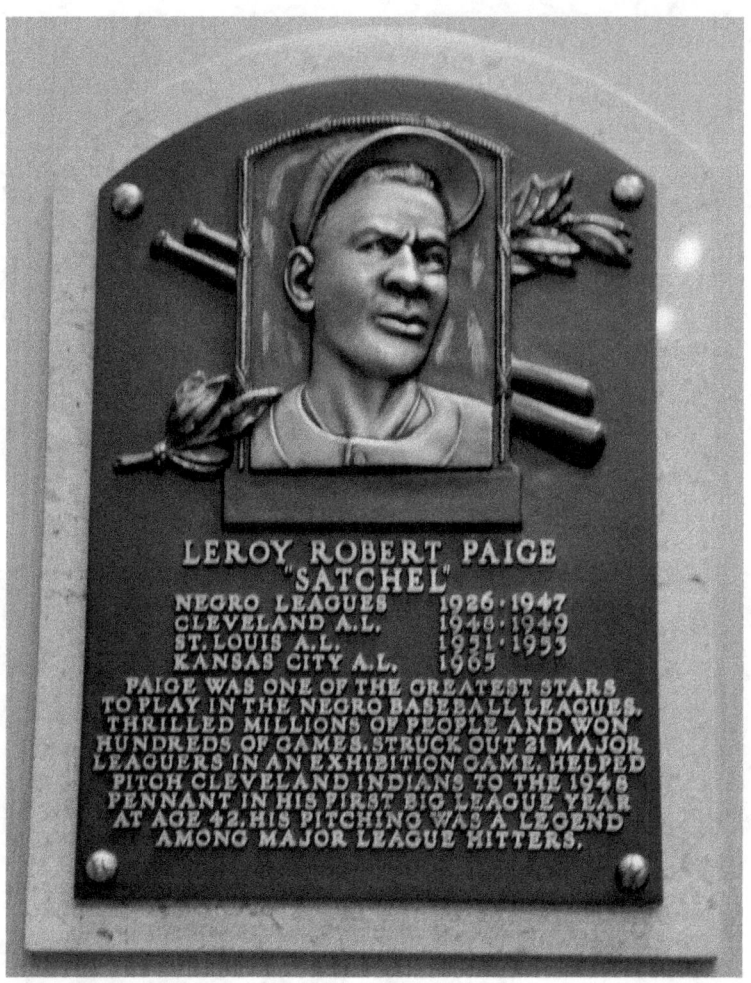

He began his professional baseball career in the Negro League with Chattanooga. He then progressed to better clubs in Birmingham, Baltimore, Cleveland, Pittsburgh and Kansas City. Paige bounced from so many teams to teams that he became known as the "Traveling Man." He loved to barnstorm in Latin America and Canada as well as in the United States with various teams. He claims to have pitched 153 games in a single season.

. . .

Many of the records from the early years of the Negro League were never kept, are lost, or are inaccurate. Because of this it is hard to ascertain much of Paige's individual records. The biggest source of Paige's legend is Paige himself. Paige claims to have pitched in more than 2,500 games with 200 shutouts. He says he struck out an average of 22 batters per game and pitched 20 no-hitters. Because of the scarcity of records, it is hard to prove his claims. Perhaps, just as importantly, it is impossible to disprove them.

During his barn-storming career, Paige played against some of the great major leaguers, including Bob Feller and Dizzy Dean. Unlike so many other Negro League players, Paige actually had a chance to play in the Major Leagues. In 1948, at the age of 42, Bill Veeck signed Paige to play for the Cleveland Indians. He played six years in the Majors with Cleveland, the St. Louis Browns and Kansas City. His record for those six years was: 28-31, with a 3.29 ERA.

Paige's fastball, like Paige himself, is also a thing of legend. He called his fastball various names: bee ball, jump ball, trouble ball and, lastly, Long Tom. Legend had it that his fastball was so fast at times when a batter swung and missed the ball never landed in the catcher's mitt. They would look around wondering where it was. Players wondered where did the ball go?

Satchel Paige ended his career in 1965 at 59 years of age.

Satchel's Stats (Negro League)
Shutouts: 27
Complete Games: 130
Innings Pitched: 1298
Wins: 100
Strikeouts: 1170
Walks: 240
Hits: 995
ERA: 3.22

Satchel's Stats (Major League)
Shutouts: 4
Innings Pitched: 476
Wins: 28
Losses: 31
Strikeouts: 288
Walks: 180
Hits: 429
ERA: 3.29

3

JOSH GIBSON

BORN: JOSHUA GIBSON on December 21, 1911 in
   Buena Vista, Georgia
DIED: January 20, 1947 in Pittsburgh, Pennsylvania
Inducted into the National Baseball Hall of Fame
   in 1972

*J*osh Gibson was referred to as the "Black Babe Ruth," in the Negro League for his prodigious home run power.

Gibson's first wore a baseball uniform when he was 16, playing for an all-Negro team sponsored by Gimbels Department Store. He began as a catcher, but eventually also played third base. The Gimbels team became part of the Negro Greater Pittsburgh Industrial League. The Pittsburgh Bath House, which recruited sponsors and later became the Pittsburgh Crawfords, was also in the league.

In 1929 and 1930, Gibson played for a semi-pro team called the Cranford Colored Giants. During the 1930 season he joined the Homestead Grays. On September 27, 1930, the Grays were playing the Lincoln Giants at Yankee Stadium. Gibson hit a monster home run into the leftfield bleachers which was estimated to have gone anywhere from 430 to 460 feet.

. . .

In 1931 Gibson knew he would be treated better in Puerto Rico than he was in the United States, due to segregation. He was paid $250 per month in Puerto Rico.

In 1933 Gibson returned to the United States and decided to play with the Pittsburgh Crawfords in the new Negro National League.

In 1936, still with the Crawfords, Gibson played another game in Yankee Stadium and stroked another epic home run. Jack Marshall, playing for the opposing team, the Chicago American Giants, swore the ball went out of the park. In 1937, Gibson played again in Yankee Stadium, and once again he hit a monster home run. The ball travelled 580 feet, according to a writer for *The Sporting News*.

In 1937, Dizzy Dean concluded, "Josh Gibson is one of the best catchers that ever caught a ball, and boy oh boy, can he hit that ball."

Gibson decided to play Winter Ball in Cuba for the 1937-38 season. He batted .342. When he returned to the United States, he decided to join the Homestead Grays again. That season he batted .365 with 10 home runs.

After playing in Cuba, Gibson got on a plane and flew to the Dominican Republic to play alongside Cool Papa Bell, Satchel Paige and Perucho Cepeda (father of Hall of Famer Orlando Cepeda). The fans, many of them sugar cane workers, crowded into the local cafes, bars and restaurants, longing to see the black players, especially Josh Gibson. The Dominican fans still speak about the 1937 season when Josh Gibson hit a titanic home run. According to Coleridge Mayer, a local fan, "It was the biggest home run I have ever seen anyone hit."

In 1939, there were a number of sportswriters who aided the black press in making it known that segregation was a dominant issue in the Major Leagues. One writer, Jimmy Powers, wrote in the *New York Daily News* that he could testify to the ability of a number of black players who should be in the Major Leagues now. Powers further stated, "I am positive (that) if Josh Gibson were white, he would be a major league star." *Washington Post* sportswriter Shirley Povich agreed, "There is a ton of talent playing in the Negro Leagues. Twenty-game winners, .350 hitters and a catcher, Josh Gibson, no doubt better than Bill Dickey. The only thing keeping him from the Major Leagues is the color of his skin. It's a boycott the majors have set up against colored players."

In 1940, Gibson decided to play Winter Ball in Mexico and Puerto Rico. Playing in Mexico, he hit 10 home runs, which tied him for second place in the Mexican League. He then left Mexico and went to Puerto Rico where he batted .480. He once again hit a gigantic home run, estimated to travel 600 feet.

In 1943, Gibson was hospitalized for seizures while playing for the Homestead Grays. Further exams revealed he had a brain tumor. Gibson refused to admit his condition and wouldn't discuss it with anyone. When he returned from the hospital, his batting became lethal. He batted, .486, and hit 12 home runs and 22 doubles.

. . .

In 1945, Josh Gibson led the Homestead Grays to another Negro National League crown, as he batted .323.

In 1946 Josh Gibson hit several noteworthy home runs. He hit a 440-foot home run in Yankee Stadium; a 457-foot home run in Pittsburgh's Forbes Field, and a 500-foot blast at Sportsman Park in St. Louis. Topping that, Gibson cleared the roof with a massive home run in Philadelphia's Shibe Park.

Josh Gibson was considered the best hitter in all of black baseball throughout his career. His great hitting helped the Homestead Grays win nine consecutive Negro League titles.

Many sportswriters believed Gibson died from a broken heart because he was unable to play in the integrated Major Leagues. Gibson's son, Josh Jr. said, "When I hear that stuff about how my father died of a broken heart, it pisses me off, because that wasn't my father. He was the last guy to brood about something he couldn't do nothing (sic) about."

After Josh Gibson died, his teammate Harold Tinker, stated, "There was no better hitter in the Negro Leagues than Josh. It's a shame he never was able to make it to the Major League. He would have been a star." People went crazy over Roy Campanella, but he was no comparison to Josh Gibson. Monte Irvin commented, "Josh Gibson was the best all-around player, and definitely the best hitter. I played with Willie Mays and against Hank Aaron, they were tremendous players, but they were no Josh Gibson."

<u>Josh Gibson's Lifetime Stats</u>:
At Bats:	1957
Batting Average:	.359
Hits:	676
Home Runs:	113
Triples:	45
Doubles:	106
Runs Batted In:	361
Walks:	158
Stolen Bases:	26

4

BUCK LEONARD

BORN: WALTER FENNER LEONARD on September 8, 1907 in Rocky Mount, North Carolina
DIED: November 27, 1997 in Rocky Mount, North Carolina
NICKNAME: "Buck"
Inducted into the Baseball Hall of Fame in 1972

Buck Leonard was considered one of the purest hitters in the Negro League. He was often referred to as the "black Lou Gehrig."

Leonard was a key player for the Homestead Grays in the 1930's & 1940's. He spent his entire 15-year career with the Homestead Grays. This is the longest any player stayed with one team in the Negro League. After joining the Homestead Grays in 1934, Leonard's consistent, superior defensive play, and his ability to hit with power and for high average, were the reasons why he was chosen to play in a Negro League record twelve East-West All- Star Games.

Baseball historian Jim Riley praised Buck Leonard's fielding and hitting, saying, "He possessed a smooth swing at the plate, (and) he was equally smooth in the field." Riley also pointed out, "Leonard was a team man all the way. A class guy, he was the best-liked player in the game."

. . .

In 1941, a media source said this about Buck Leonard: "While Josh Gibson was slugging tape measure home runs, Leonard was hitting screaming line drives off the outfield wall and over them ... Trying to sneak a fastball past him was like trying to sneak a sunrise past a rooster."

At age 45, Buck Leonard was offered a Major League contract, but he turned it down. He said, "In 1952, I knew I was over the hill." He admitted, "I didn't try to fool myself." When Clark Griffith, owner of the Washington Senators, asked Leonard and Gibson if they would like to play in the Major Leagues, both said "Yes." Then Griffith asked, "Do you think you can hit Major League pitching?" Leonard said, "We'll hit some, and some we won't." At that point Griffith told both, "The reason why we haven't got you colored ball players on the team, the time hasn't come for you to be integrated."

Buck Leonard played in four consecutive Negro World Series (1941-1944) with the Homestead Grays. The Homestead Grays won the Negro World Series in 1941 and 1944.

In 1951, 1952 and 1953 Buck Leonard went to Mexico to play Winter Ball. He was happy to report, "The money was great and the people treated us well."

<u>Buck Leonard's Lifetime stats</u>:

At Bats:	1439
Batting Average:	.320
Hits:	476
Home Runs:	57
Triples:	26
Doubles:	74
Runs Scored:	352
Runs Batted In:	251
Walks:	162
Stolen Bases:	27

5

MONTE IRVIN

BORN: MONTFORD MERRILL IRVIN on February
25, 1919 in Haleberg, Alabama
DIED: January 11, 2016 in Houston, Texas
Inducted into the National Baseball Hall of Fame
in 1973

*I*f Monte Irvin had followed his father's wishes, we may have known about him as a famous musician, and would probably have never seen him play baseball. Irvin's father gave him money to buy a saxophone, but young Monte saw a baseball glove in a store window and bought that instead. Soon thereafter he began playing centerfield for the Newark Eagles.

Irvin attended Orange High School and was a four-sport athlete, playing football, basketball, baseball and running track. In his senior year in high school, Irvin was signed to play for the Newark Eagles of the Negro National League. He actually played under an assumed name, Jimmy Nelson, to protect his amateur status, allowing him to continue playing in high school and college.

Irvin played shortstop and third base on the Eagles. Larry Doby played second base. Doby and Irvin would later again play together for the New York Giants in the Major Leagues.

In 1942 Irvin left the Eagles to play Winter ball in Mexico to make more money. He batted .317 with 20 home runs. Irvin referred to this year in Mexico as the best time of his life. He said, "I felt wanted and free. I could go anywhere, eat anywhere, and stay in any hotel I wanted, just like anyone else. It was wonderful."

Irvin served in the United States Army from 1943-46 during World War II. His unit was deployed in England and France. They built bridges and roads for the U.S. troops and their allies. He remembered, "My unit was of all blacks, except for the officers who were white. We weren't treated badly, but could have been better."

On September 1, 1945 Irvin was discharged from the Army. He returned to play baseball with the Newark Eagles. Prior to the war, he hit .400, but after the war he only hit .300. Missing those three years took a lot out of him.

Irving was batting .404 when the Newark Eagles made it into the playoffs. They eventually beat the Kansas City Monarchs in the Negro World Series. Irvin batted .462 against Satchel Paige and Hilton Smith.

Many black players thought Monte Irvin should have been called to the Major Leagues before Jackie Robinson. Finally, in 1949 Monte Irvin was called up to the Major Leagues by the New York Giants. He was somewhat bitter, complaining, "This should have happened ten years ago. I am not half the ballplayer I was then." Roy Campanella agreed, saying, "Monte was the best all-around ballplayer I have ever seen. As great as he was in 1951, he was twice as good ten years earlier in the Negro Leagues."

Monte Irvin had an inspiring career in the Negro League. He was a tremendous power hitter, batting .289 in 1939. He then followed with seasons of .351 and a league-leading .397 in 1941. Irvin led the Newark Eagles to the Negro League title in 1946, batting a league-high .383. During this career in the Negro League, Irvin was selected to play in six East-West All-Star games.

Irvin has the proud distinction, shared only by one other Negro League player, Martin Dihigo, of membership in the Halls of Fame of four countries - Mexico, Cuba, Puerto Rico and the United States.

Working tirelessly to keep the black league alive, Monte Irvin has always been supportive of all the men who played in black baseball in the Negro Leagues. In every way, Monte Irvin is a champion all his life.

On July 8, 1949, Irvin and Hank Thompson arrived in New York to play for the Giants. Leo Durocher was the manager. He told them, "With you two guys on the team we should win the World Series."

In 1951 Irvin batted .312, with 24 home runs and 121 RBI's. He finished third in the Most Valuable Player voting behind Roy Campanella and Stan Musial. That year the Giants made it into the World Series and played the New York Yankees. Irvin tied a record by batting .458 in the Series. In one game Irvin stole home against Allie Reynolds. Unfortunately for him and his fellow Giants, the Yankees won the World Series. Irvin went on to have a fantastic season in 1952. He batted .329 with 97 RBI's. In the last game, Irvin accomplished what very few players have done - he was safe stealing home.

In 1954 Durocher's prophecy finally came through when the Giants finally won the World Series by beating the heavily-favored Cleveland Indians. It was in Game 1 when Irvin was playing left field and observed Willie Mays playing center field and making a sensational catch on a deep drive off the bat of Vic Wertz. The Giants won four straight games to win their first World Series since 1933.

The 1954 World Series included twelve eventual Hall of Famers - umpires, players and managers. They were umpires Al Barlick and Jocko Conlan, managers Leo Durocher and Al Lopez, and players Monte Irvin, Willie Mays, Larry Doby, Bob Lemon, Early Wynn, Hal Newhouser and Bob Feller.

Cormac Gordon, sportswriter for the *Staten Island Advance*, reported this about Irvin. "Irvin was without a doubt one of the first outstanding black players in the major leagues and a Hall of Famer for his brillance with the Negro League, where he spent most of his prime years before baseball's color barrier was shattered." Gordon went on to state, "On the baseball field playing for the New York Giants, Irvin hit for both average and power. He also was a base stealer and cut down runners from the outfield with his howitzer of a right arm. By the time he played his first game for the Giants in 1949, after years as a star for the Newark Eagles of the Negro National League, having endured long bus rides, rundown hotels and the precarious paydays of black baseball, he was already 30, two years older than Jackie Robinson had been when Robinson broke the major league color line with the Brooklyn Dodgers."

Irvin knew his best years were behind him. "I was past my peak then," he said, "My only regret is that I didn't get the shot when I was 19, when I was a real ballplayer."

Most black ballplayers thought Monte Irvin should have been first in the Major Leagues. Cool Papa Bell reminisced, "Monte was our best young ballplayer at the time. He could hit that long ball, had a great arm, he could field, he could run. Yes, he could do it all."

When Monte Irvin retired, he became baseball's first black executive in 1968, when he was named to handle promotion and public relations for Commissioner William D. Eckert. He remained in the commissioner's office, as an aide to Eckert's successor, Bowie Kuhn, until 1968.

On January 11, 2016, Monte Irvin died at the ripe old age of 96.

<u>Irvin's Lifetime Major League Stats</u>:

Games Played:	764
At Bats:	2499
Batting Average:	.293
Hits:	731
Home Runs:	99
Triples:	31
Doubles:	97
Runs Scored:	366
Runs Batted In:	443

<u>Negro League Stats</u>:

At Bats:	570
Batting Average:	.354
Hits:	202
Home Runs:	20
Triples:	7
Doubles:	27
Runs Scored:	1127
Runs Batted In:	135

6

COOL PAPA BELL

BORN: JAMES THOMAS NICHOLS on May 17, 1903 in Starkville, Mississippi
DIED: JANUARY 20, 1991 in St. Louis, Missouri
Inducted into the Baseball Hall of Fame in 1974

"Cool Papa" Bell was a fast runner and a great hitter. Ironically, his first game in the Negro League was in 1922 as the pitcher for the East St. Louis Stars against the Indianapolis ABC's. He received the nickname "Cool Papa" from his manager, Bill Gatewood. At the time, the St. Louis Stars were in a tough game when Bell struck out Oscar Charleston. Gatewood commented, "He's Cool" - and added "Papa" to it.

Bell's speed was so legendary he was referred to as the "Black Ty Cobb." Bell played the outfield for the Stars when he wasn't pitching. In one game he circled the bases in 13.6 seconds. Fellow players said, "He's faster than a country mile," but it was Buck O'Neil who really summed up Bell's speed. Whenever O'Neil was asked how fast Cool Papa Bell was, he would reply, "Faster than that." But of course, it was Satchel Paige who famously said, "Bell was so fast he could flip the light switch and jump into bed before the lights go out."

"Cool Papa" Bell was noted throughout the Negro League as a jokester. Here is an example of one he played on Satchel Paige. Paige told this story numerous times over the years as he thought it was true. But it was during a Negro League reunion that Bell finally came clean.

• • •

Here's Bell's story. "During the winter season in the 1930's, Satchel and I roomed together in California. One night, before he returned to the room, I turned off the light, but the light didn't go out right away. There was a delay of about three seconds from the time I flipped the switch and the light went out. There must have been a short or something. I thought to myself, here's a chance fool ol' Satch. He always played tricks on everybody else. Anyway, he came back to the room and I said, 'Hey Satch, I'm pretty fast, right?' 'You the fastest,' he said. 'Well,' I said, 'you haven't seen anything yet. Why, I'm so fast, I can turn out the light and be in bed before the light goes out.' 'Sure Cool, sure you can.' I told him to sit down and watch. I turned off the light, jumped in bed, and pulled the covers up to my chin. Then the lights went out. I howled and Satch was speechless for once. Anyway, he has been telling the truth all these years."

Bill Veeck thought, "Bell is as good as Willie Mays, Joe DiMaggio and Tris Speaker."

Bell enjoyed barnstorming, especially when he went to Latin America. He said, "Everyone was the same down there. We could go to restaurants, stay in hotels and, oh those fans, they loved us." Life in Latin America was a stark contrast to the way Negro League players were treated under the Jim Crow Laws in the States. Bell remained in the Mexico League 1938-1940.

When Bell retired in 1945, he remained in baseball managing the Monarch Travelers until 1949. He was adept at recognizing future stars. He recommended Ernie Banks to Buck O'Neil, who placed Banks on the Kansas City Monarchs.

• • •

Bell's Final Stats in 1945 was .368 BA in 159 games; 16 Hr.'s; 12 triples; 31 doubles, and he was unanimously elected into the Baseball Hall of Fame in 1974.

<u>Bell's Lifetime Stats</u>:

Games Played:	848
At Bats:	3378
Batting Average:	.316
Hits:	1066
Home Runs:	33
Triples:	51
Doubles:	152
Runs Scored:	717
Runs Batted In:	211
Walks:	318
Stolen Bases:	167

WILLIAM "JUDY" JOHNSON

BORN: William Julius Johnson on October 26, 1899 at Snow Hill, Maryland
DIED: June 15, 1989 at Wilmington, Delaware.
NICKNAME: "JUDY"
Inducted into the Baseball Hall of Fame in 1975

Judy Johnson's father wanted him to become a boxer. He rejected his Dad's wishes as he had aspirations to become a professional baseball player.

Judy's nickname came about as there was a Judy Gans on the same team and Judy Johnson resembled Gans. But because Judy Johnson was on the team before Gans, Johnson remained with the nickname.

In 1921, Judy Johnson signed with the Hilldale club of the Negro League as a third baseman. He played with Hilldale from

1921-1929. His best season was in 1929 when his BA was .365 and 72 RBI's.

He also played winter ball in Florida and Cuba because, as he said, "The money was too good to let go by." Judy's Winter League playing days in Cuba ran from 1926-1931. His best season was in 1927 when he batted .333.

. . .

Johnson eventually became the best third baseman in the Negro Leagues. Teammate Ted Page felt that, "Judy Johnson was the smartest third baseman I ever came across." Another teammate, Willie Wells, added to that by agreeing that, "Johnson had intelligence and finesse on the field and at bat."

Johnson was a mentor to Josh Gibson who called Johnson "Jing." Gibson felt strongly that, "He made a better player of me."

The legendary Connie Mack even offered his opinion that, "If Judy Johnson were white, he would write his own price."

Judy Johnson became the first African American scout in the Major Leagues when he was hired by the Philadelphia Athletics. He scouted many black players for the Athletics and also scouted for the Milwaukee Brewers. His longest tenure as a scout was 1959 to 1974, when he scouted for the Philadelphia Phillies.

His teammate Ted Page felt that Johnson's talents were underutilized, feeling "He should have been in the major leagues 15 or 20 years as a coach." Page added, "They talk about Negro managers. If he were a manager, he would have done wonders developing young talent in the major leagues."

Many of his teammates, and even his opponents, agreed that, "Johnson would make an excellent manager in the Major Leagues."

<u>Johnson's Lifetime stats</u>:

Games played:	780
At bats:	2990
Batting Average:	.293
Hits:	876
Home Runs:	26
Triples:	46
Doubles:	121
Runs scored:	590
Walks:	149
Stolen bases:	73

8

OSCAR CHARLESTON

*BORN: OSCAR McKINLEY CHARLESTON on
October 14, 1896 at Indianapolis, Indiana
DIED: October 5, 1954 at home due to falling down
stairs
Inducted into the National Baseball Hall of Fame
in 1976*

At 15 years of age, Oscar Charleston lied about his age and entered the United States Army. He was stationed in the Philippines, where he played for the regimental baseball team. He was selected to the All-Star Team, where he pitched a one-hit shutout and hit a triple. Oscar was honorably discharged from the Army in 1915.

He returned to the States and began playing in the Negro League with the Indianapolis ABC's, but he had a bad temper and was released from the team. Ironically, many players thought he was a charismatic figure, right from the start when he joined the Indianapolis ABC's in 1915 to 1954, the year he managed the Indianapolis Clowns to a championship - before his tragic death..

After being released by the Indianapolis ABC's, Oscar decided to play Winter Ball in Cuba. He didn't last long on the team again, because of his bad temper and his disobedience of club rules. Oscar's personality was that of an argumentative and belligerent person. He tangled with umpires, Klu Klux Klansmen and Cuban soldiers - but when it came to the younger players, he was a sweetheart, and the players appreciated his counsel. He not only encompassed the Negro League; he symbolized the Negro Leagues with his heart and his spirit and his talent.

Oscar played on two of the best teams in the Negro League. The best were the 1931 Homestead Grays and the 1935 Pittsburgh Crawfords.

He went to New York to play with the Lincoln Stars, but only for half of the season. Oscar then got a reprieve, returning to play with the Indianapolis ABC's in August 1916. In October, the ABC's played Rube Foster's American Giants in a seven-game series which was dubbed the Black Baseball Championship. The ABC's won the series and championship behind the hitting of Oscar Charleston who batted 7 for 18 (.388).

In 1917, the United States became involved in World War I and Charleston then registered for the draft. In order to maintain consistency with his previous lie when he first entered the Army, he lied about his date of birth, telling the authorities he was born on October 14, 1893. He was supposed to enter Colored Students Officer Training School but the War ended and he received his second honorable discharge.

Because of his power as a hitter, Charleston was often

referred to as the "Black Babe Ruth." He played a lot like Ty Cobb, covered more ground than grass, and ran like the wind.

Buck O'Neil commented, "If I had to name the best all-around player in the Negro League, without a doubt, it would be Oscar Charleston." Many believed he was a better player than Rogers Hornsby because of his hitting, speed and exceptional fielding.

During Oscar Charleston's career in one season of 53 games he compiled a batting average of .318, with 11 home runs. This was done against Major League players. He got hits off Walter Johnson, Bob Feller and Lefty Grove.

When he was playing Winter Ball in Cuba, Charleston finished the season with a .446 batting average, but was denied the batting title because his team, Santa Clara, withdrew prior to the season ending. The team officials withdrew because the league took away one of their wins.

Oscar Charleston's Stats:
Games Played:	824
At Bats:	3981
Batting Average:	.339
Hits:	1350
Home Runs:	141
Triples:	89
Doubles:	219
Runs Batted In:	624

9

MARTIN DIHIGO

BORN: May 25, 1925 in Matanzas, Cuba
DIED: May 20, 1971 in Cienfuegos, Cuba
NICKNAME: "El Maestro"
Inducted into the National Baseball Hall of Fame
in 1977

Martin Dihigo was an unknown to North American baseball fans, owners of Major League teams and scouts. Why? Well, playing in Cuba and the Caribbean leagues didn't help his baseball credentials from reaching beyond those islands, because of the existence of communism.

When Castro came to power, he immediately abolished the Cuban Baseball League, making Dihgo even more unknown. It wasn't until Negro League and Major League players were permitted to barnstorm into Latin American countries, including Cuba, that Martin Dihigo finally became noticed for his baseball prowess.

Dihigo was a national treasure to the Cuban fans. They knew of his great baseball abilities and accomplishment on the diamond. Before the Castro regime came to power, the Cuban fans concurred Dihigo was the best ballplayer their island ever produced.

In Cuba, before communism and the rise of amateur sports, Dihigo was acknowledged everywhere as Babe Ruth, Joe DiMaggio and Walter Johnson all wrapped up in one. Imagine, an athlete who played all over the diamond and was skillful at every position. That person was Martin Dihigo - baseball's greatest all-around Negro Leaguer in the eyes of old-timers and top talent in every corner of the planet.

Dihigo was noticed for the first time while pitching in Mexico on September 5, 1938. Under intense heat, he outdueled and outpitched Satchel Paige in a barnstorming game which eventually ended in the 9th inning when Dihigo blasted a walk-off home run. His team, Aquilla, beat Paige's team, Amario.

On the Amario team, besides Paige, were future Hall of Famers Josh Gibson, Ray Dandridge and Willie Wells.

In Mexico, where Dihigo played the infield when he wasn't on the mound, he had a lifetime batting average of .317. In eleven seasons of Winter Ball in Cuba, where he played mostly as a pitcher, Dihigo's career batting average was over .300 with 130 home runs.

Buck Leonard remembered, "I witnessed Dihigo slam a monster home run at Pittsburgh's Greenlee Field. The ball traveled over 500 feet, landing on the roof of the hospital across the street from the field.

Others described Dihigo as having wrists as strong as Ernie Banks and Hank Aaron, which they believed enabled him to be a fierce hitter, one of the best in the Negro League.

Martin Dihigo at age 43 decided to play and manage a baseball team in the Dominican Republic. On the team was

Johnny Mize, who starred with the New York Giants. Mize once said, "Dihigo is the greatest baseball player I have ever seen. He should have been in the Major Leagues."

In reality, Dihigo didn't become well-known until he was inducted into the Baseball Hall of Fame in 1977. He is the only player who also was inducted into five Halls of Fame - the United States, Mexico, Venezuela, Cuba and the Dominican Republic.

Because of his prowess on the field, hitting, pitching and fielding, the people of Cuba nicknamed him "El Maestro," surely a fitting and well-deserved moniker.

Dihigo Lifetime Stats (Pitcher)

Games Started:	36
Complete Games:	28
Innings Pitched:	339
Wins:	23
Losses:	20
Shutouts:	1
Strikeouts:	158
Walks:	69
ERA:	2.29

Lifetime Stats (Player)

At Bats:	1404
Batting Average:	.307
Hits:	431
Home Runs:	64
Triples:	17
Doubles:	61
Runs Scored:	292
Runs Batted In:	227
Walks:	143
Stolen Bases:	41

10

POP LLOYD

BORN: *JOHN HENRY LLOYD on April 25, 1884 at Palatka, Florida*
DIED: *March 19, 1964 at Atlantic City, New Jersey*
NICKNAME: *"Pop"*
Inducted into the Baseball Hall of Fame in 1977

Lloyd didn't begin to play baseball until 1904 when he was 20 years old because of the Jim Crow laws in effect in the South. He was interested, and determined to become a baseball player. He tried out and made a semi-pro team, the Jacksonville Young Receivers, as a catcher. Eventually he moved to Macon, Georgia, where he joined a semi-pro team called the Acmes. He soon learned the management of the team couldn't afford to purchase a mask or chest protector for Lloyd. He was so determined to become a professional player, he remained on the team. Lloyd, playing his first game without a mask or chest protector, received a black eye. Being innovative, he went home and made a mask from a wire basket. The mask lasted the entire season.

Lloyd left the Acmes team in 1906, determined to play for a professional team. He tried out and joined the Cuban X Giants of the Negro League. He remained playing for twelve different teams in his career, which lasted until 1932. It was during this period Lloyd switched from catching to playing shortstop. The last team he played for was the Philadelphia Giants.

. . .

Sol White, the manager of the Lincoln Giants, was in need of a good shortstop. He was told about Pop Lloyd and convinced Lloyd to join his team.

Connie Mack saw Lloyd play numerous times, and commented, "Lloyd and Honus Wagner are two of the best shortstops to play in the Negro League."

Lloyd was on the move again. In 1918 he became a manager for the first time in his career, managing the Brooklyn Royal Giants. He also played first base, realizing, "I was in my 40's, and not as quick and agile enough to play shortstop."

Lloyd only remained with the Brooklyn Royal Giants for a short time, when he left to manage these various teams: the Columbus Ohio Buckeyes, Bacharach Giants, Hilldale Club and the Lincoln Giants. It was Sol White who convinced Lloyd to manage the Lincoln Giants, as White was retiring.

Judy Johnson, playing for the Hilldale Club in 1923, remembered, "Lloyd was a great man, motivator and teacher of the game. We truly enjoyed playing for him, as he taught us how to play the game hard, with a determination to win when we took the field."

Lloyd's best stats were in 1911, when he had a .375 batting average at the age of 27. Then, at the age of 39, he batted .418. Many sportswriters witnessed Lloyd playing shortstop through the years and were convinced he was one of the greatest in the Negro League.

Lloyd decided to retire in 1932, but was asked to manage

the Newark Eagles and also the Baltimore Elite Giants. He refused both offers.

He was comfortable in retirement, working for the United States Post Office in Atlantic City, New Jersey. He decided to teach youths how to play baseball and to be good citizens. Lloyd enjoyed working with the children, as he never had children of his own.

<u>Lloyd's Lifetime Stats</u>:

Games:	332
At Bats:	3159
Batting Average:	.337
Hits:	1066
Home Runs:	22
Triples:	44
Doubles:	151
Runs Scored:	532
Runs Batted In:	350
Walks:	196
Stolen Bases:	97

11

RUBE FOSTER

BORN: ANDREW FOSTER on September 17, 1879 at
Calvert, Texas
DIED: December 9, 1930 at Kankakee, Illinois
NICKNAME: "Rube"
Inducted into the National Baseball Hall of Fame
in 2001

Jackie Robinson is considered to have the greatest impact on integration in baseball. But it is understood as well that the greatest impact upon African-American baseball was Rube Foster. He was considered the greatest pitcher and eventual manager in the early twentieth century. He was given the proud distinction as the "Architect of Negro National League."

Foster faced immense racial prejudice, but he persisted to carry out three distinct positions during his lifetime, and for these reasons is often known as the "Father of Negro Baseball." He, along with his half-brother, William "Bill" Foster, were inducted into the National Baseball Hall of Fame.

Foster joined the Cuban X Giants in 1903. He became an excellent pitcher, leading the X Giants to a championship. No less than Honus Wagner effused, "Foster is one of the greatest pitchers of all time." Foster once taught the great Christy Mathewson how to throw a screwball.

. . .

Foster began his player/manager career in 1907 with the Leland Giants under the ownership of Frank Leland. The Giants won 110 games and captured the Chicago City title. As a manager, Foster's pet hitting play was the "bunt & run," which he taught to his players.

He began a barnstorming schedule with the Leland Giants, which was his trademark for the next decade. On February 20,1907, the *Indianapolis Freeman* reported that the Leland Giants would embark on a spring training tour.

They played white semi-pro clubs in Milwaukee, Chicago and Joliet, Illinois, leading the newspapers to report the Leland Giants were about to break that strong barrier of racial prejudice.

The Leland Giants benefitted from several top white semi-pro clubs in the Windy City playing them. Rivalries began to emerge with the Logan Squares, Adrian Anson's Colts and Jake Stahl's South Chicagos. Because of Foster and the Leland Giants originating the barnstorming tour, several black teams from the South barnstormed to the Midwest during the regular season.

For his efforts, when Rube Foster returned to his home state of Texas, they gave him a hero's welcome. His reception in Fort Worth would "have done honor to the President of the United States." In Houston, the Lelands played to the largest crowd ever at a baseball game in that city. The Giants swept the local Texas club in three games to win the series.

A large contingent from Foster's hometown of Calvert attended one of the games. Like the Page Fence Giants before them, the Leland Giants traveled in a Pullman sleeper, thus avoiding the prejudices of white hotel managers in the South.

On July 6, 1907, the *Broad Ax* (local newspaper) reported that the Leland Giants and the Birmingham Giants would play a two-game series, and a $500 side bet was placed on the eventual winner. The Leland Giants swept the series.

Rube Foster suffered a serious leg injury during a game in 1909 which sidelined him. As a result, the Giants lost a crucial championship.

Soon after, Foster attempted to wrest control of the Giants from Leland but to no avail.

In 1910, Foster left the Leland Giants to put together his own team, the American Giants. He formed the Giants with players from the Leland Giants and Philadelphia Giants. On the team were John "Pop" Lloyd, Pete Hill and Home Run Johnson. Foster was able to return to pitching again, leading the American Giants to a record, 128 wins and 6 losses.

Foster began having health problems in 1926 due to his exposure to a form of toxic gas. The exposure led to Foster suffering from loss of memory and behavioral problems. As a result, he was confined to an asylum, where he eventually passed away. This was a sad ending for a man about whom author Robert Peterson said, "If the talents of Christy Mathewson, John McGraw, Ben Johnson and Judge Kennesaw Mountain Landis were combined to a single body, and that body was enveloped into black skin, the result would be named Andrew "Rube" Foster.

RAY DANDRIDGE

BORN: August 31, 1913 at Richmond, Virginia
DIED: February 12, 1994 at Palm Bay, Florida
Inducted into the Baseball Hall of Fame in 1987

Ray Dandridge was considered one of the greatest third baseman to ever play in the Negro League. In the late 1930's Dandridge played for the Detroit Stars, the Newark Eagles, Newark Dodgers and New York Cubans in the Negro League.

When Dandridge played for the Newark Eagles, the infield was called "the million dollar" infield. It consisted of Dandridge, Willie Wells, Dick Seay and Mule Suttles. His teammates remembered, "Ray Dandridge was so bow-legged a freight train could fit between his legs, but you couldn't get a ground ball past him. Dandridge was selected to play in three East-West All-Star Games.

Dandridge played a total of ten years of Winter Ball in Cuba, Puerto Rico, Mexico and Venezuela. This was a practical decision he made due to the discrimination prevalent. Dandridge related that, "I played in foreign countries because of the Jim Crow Laws in the States treating black ball players badly." In explaining why he left the Newark Eagles to play in other countries, Dandridge said that it "was because the foreign countries, the places we went to, paid my expenses, my family's expenses, gave us an apartment and everything. If we stayed with the Eagles, we'd have nothing." He explained that "I stayed in Mexico for seven years. All my expenses were paid - my wife, my kids, my transportation. Besides, my money was clear there. When I left Mexico, I would go play in Cuba, where we were treated just as good. They put my kids in school and everything else was taken care of, just like in Mexico."

Another reason for the lure to Mexico of the Negro League players was the Mexican League president, Jorge Pasquel, who was a liquor mogul with political connections. He offered the Negro players salaries that no Negro League team could come close to. These players, Ray Dandridge, Josh Gibson, Willie Wells, Johnny Taylor and Ray Brown were put up in the finest hotels, and adored by the sporting public. Many of these players considered their playing in Mexico the best in their career. Many white Major League players were also lured by Paquel, such as Sal Maglie, Max Lanier and Mickey Owens.

The Major Leagues were cherry-picking the most promising young players from the Negro American League - and some were not so young. Ray Dandridge for example, told the Minneapolis Millers, a farm team of the New York Giants, that he was 29 years old, when in fact he was 36 years old. He batted .364 and was second in the balloting for the American Association Rookie of the Year.

The following year he was the league's Most Valuable Player. Despite this achievement, Dandridge was never called up to the parent New York Giants roster. Monte Irvin, a New York Giant, was saddened that, "Dandridge didn't play in the Major League, but had the talent. He sure was a superstar."
Many other talented players were signed to lower minor league teams by their parent Major League teams. Historian

Jules Tygiel concluded, "Generally underestimating the quality of play in the Negro Leagues, baseball officials placed most of the new recruits in classifications far beneath their talent. As a result, blacks compiled astounding statistics in the early years of integration."

Dandridge Lifetime stats:

Batting Average:	.310
At bats:	833
Runs scored:	122
Hits:	258
Doubles	31
Triples	13
Home runs:	2
Runs Batted In:	44
Stolen bases:	14
Walks:	22

13

LEON DAY

BORN: October 30, 1916 in Alexandria, Virginia
DIED: March 14, 1995 in Baltimore, Maryland
Inducted into the National Baseball Hall of Fame
   in 1995

*A*t an early age, Leon Day dreamt one day he would be in the Baseball Hall of Fame. His dream came through before he died.

Day was a pitcher and, by all accounts, a great one. Leon Day threw as hard as any pitcher in the Negro League, his fastball speeding in at 90 to 95 miles per hour. He also had a tremendous curve. In Monte Irvin's opinion, "Leon Day was a great pitcher, as good as Satchel Paige." A Newark Eagle teammate once said, "If Satchel Paige was an icon in the Negro League, then Leon Day is the warrior." Another teammate on the Newark Eagles commented, "I didn't see anyone better than Leon Day."

On August 1, 1943, 51,723 spectators packed Chicago's Comiskey Park to watch a Negro League East-West All-Star Game. Day was part of the game with some of the greatest stars ever to play this game, including Monte Irvin, Buck O'Neil, Josh

Gibson, Satchel Paige and "Double Duty" Radcliffe. Two weeks prior to this game the white Major Leaguers played their All-Star Game and only drew 32,000 fans. The fact that the Negro League outdrew the majors was no singular event. Between 1938 and 1948, the Negro League East-West All-Star Game outdrew the major league All-Star Game seven times. The reason for this was because players like Leon Day, Josh Gibson and several other Black players were every bit as good as the white ball players.

In 1946, Day, pitching for the Newark Eagles and threw a no-hitter against the Philadelphia Stars. Later that season the Eagles win the Negro League World Series with a come from behind 3-2 victory over the Kansas City Monarchs. Day was joined on that championship team by Monte Irvin, Larry Doby and Max Manning. Manning would be awarded the Negro National League equivalent of the Cy Young Award as the best pitcher for the season.

One day, Leon commented to a teammate that, "I never thought I would be getting paid to play baseball. I would have played for no money." When Leon Day wasn't pitching, he either played second base or the outfield.

Buck O'Neil scouted Leon Day for the Kansas City Royals, and offered this evaluation: "Day has a great arm, speed, accuracy, strikeout pitcher, very desirable."

Leon Day was not afraid to throw a "chin-whiskers" pitch to a one-armed player. He reflected, "One day the team was down in Ocean City, New Jersey. We had to play a game there. The other team had a player, Pete Gray. He was a one-armed player. He was their lead-off hitter, and the first time he came to bat we kind of looked around nonchalantly and he got a hit off me. He's standing on first base and I look over at him and said, 'I'll tell you what. Wait till you get up the next time.' I guess it was the third or fourth inning he came to bat again, and I threw right up under his neck, and he didn't get a hit the rest of the night." During this same game, Day struck out MVP Roy Campanella three times..

Leon Day was not just a great baseball pitcher for the Newark Eagles; he was a great citizen as well. He was drafted into the United States Army during World War II. It's ironic that Jim Crow Laws in the United States at that time prohibited blacks from integrating with whites. Most pointedly, they were not allowed to play in the Major Leagues at that time. But yet, they were drafted and mandated to enter the military service.

Leon Day was stationed in France during the war, serving with the 818th Amphibian Battalion. This unit's main assignment was to supply U.S. troops with provisions on Utah Beach, both during and after the D-Day invasion of Normandy. Leon Day was honorably discharged from the military and returned to the United States where he once again began playing baseball with the Newark Eagles, the team he played for prior to entering the military.

As his playing days were coming to an end, Day was hospitalized, suffering from diabetes and heart problems. Years later, while in the hospital with his wife, family members, friends and teammates visiting, he received a phone call on March 8, 1995 informing him that he was to be inducted into the Hall of Fame. Leon commented to those present, "I was so happy with the news, I didn't know what to do, I never thought this would come." Leon's wife delivered his acceptance speech at the

Cooperstown Hall of Fame induction. She was unable to finish the speech as she became too emotional.

Cormac Gordon, sportswriter for the *Staten Island Advance*, a local newspaper, wrote, "When Leon Day died in 1995, he didn't leave enough resources for his wife, Geraldine, to buy medicine in her old age."

<u>Day's Lifetime stats</u>:

Games Started:	62
Games Completed:	33
Shutouts:	3
No-Hitters:	1
Innings Pitched:	427
Runs Allowed:	142
Wins:	33
Losses:	16
Strikeouts:	264
Walks:	110
ERA:	4.51

14

BILL FOSTER

BORN: WILLIAM HENDRICK FOSTER on June 12, 1904 in Calvert, Texas
DIED: September 16, 1978 in Alcorn, Mississippi
Inducted into the Baseball Hall of Fame in 1996

Larry Lester, the current chairman of the Society for American Baseball Research's Negro League Committee, said, "Foster was to baseball what Picasso was to painting." Buck O'Neil agreed, "Foster was a front-line starter with a hard sinker, fastball and over the top curveball." These last two pitches were both strikeout pitches.

Bill Foster was considered the best lefthanded pitcher in the Negro Leagues. In 1926, while playing for the Chicago American Giants, the 22-year-old Foster pitched complete games in both games of a doubleheader against the Kansas City Monarchs. At 29 wins and 4 losses, he had the best record in the Negro League that year.

Cum Posey, owner of the Homestead Grays, effused, " Bill Foster was tall, and as a young pitcher in the 1920's, he was noted for a burning fastball." As he got older, he turned "cute," saving his fastball for when it was really needed. Bill Yancey remembers, "The guy would give up 10 hits and still shut you out. He could really pitch." In joining the American Giants, Foster went on to win hundreds of games for them until 1937. He didn't pitch this entire time with the Giants. He left in 1931 and played for the Homestead Grays and Kansas City Monarchs.

. . .

For part of the 1933 season, he played for a white semi-pro team in Jamestown, South Dakota where, in a post-season tournament, he lost to Satchel Paige and Bismark, North Dakota, 3-2.

Dave Malarcher, Foster's teammate and manager during most of his years with the American Giants, said, "Willie Foster's greatness was that he had this terrific speed and great, fast-breaking curveball and a drop ball, and he was really a master of the change-of-pace. He could throw you a real hard one, but the next pitch with the same motion would come in and strike you out, putting you to sleep. He was really a great pitcher."

On September 10, 1933, the inaugural East-West All-Star Classic was played before a rain-soaked crowd of nearly 20,000 fans. Bill Foster was chosen to play with Oscar Charleston, Josh Gibson, Judy Johnson, Mules Suttles, Willie Wells and Turkey Stearnes. Mules Suttles hit the first home run in the Classic. Over the next 20 years, the East-West All-Star Classic attracted 10,000 fans each season. Besides the Classic being played in Comiskey Park, it was also played in Griffith Stadium, Washington, D.C., Yankee Stadium, New York and Municipal Stadium, Cleveland. The game became so popular, a second game was scheduled in some seasons.

In 1923, Foster played for Arkansas. His manager at that time was his half-brother, and fellow Hall of Famer, Rube Foster.

Foster journeyed to Cuba in 1927-28 to play Winter Ball. Oscar Charleston and Judy Johnson, two future Hall-of Famers, were on his team. Foster led the league with nine complete games and two shutouts.

He returned from Cuba and signed with the Philadelphia Royal Giants. He played for them in 1928, 1931 and 1932. His record for those three years was 6-0, 9-1, and 9-0.

Bill Foster decided to retire after the 1938 season, playing with a white semi-pro team in Elgin, Illinois and the Washington Browns, a Yakima, Washington, Negro team. He returned home to become Dean and Coach of the men's baseball team at Alcorn College in Mississippi.

Bill Foster's Hall of Fame plaque has the words, "Foster was one of the best lefthanded pitchers in Negro League history."

Foster's Lifetime Stats:
Games Started:	239
Games Completed:	180
Shutouts:	30
Innings Pitched:	1675
Wins:	128
Losses:	63
Strikeouts:	987
Walks:	511
ERA:	2.40

15

WILLIE WELLS

BORN: August 19, 1906 at Austin, Texas
DIED: January 22, 1989 at Austin, Texas
NICKNAME: "THE DEVIL"
Inducted into the Baseball Hall of Fame in 1997.

He played shortstop in the Negro League and Latin American League. He played on the following teams: St. Louis Stars, St. Louis Giants, Homestead Grays, Detroit Wolves, Kansas City Monarchs, Newark Eagles, Birmingham Eagles, Baltimore/Washington Elite Giants and Memphis Red Sox.

Wells played in Veracruz and Mexico City in 1941-1944. His BA was .320. He stated, "I enjoyed playing in Mexico not only to make more money, but I was treated like a king." He didn't face racial problems as he did in the United States playing baseball. He was also inducted in the Mexican Professional Baseball Hall of Fame.

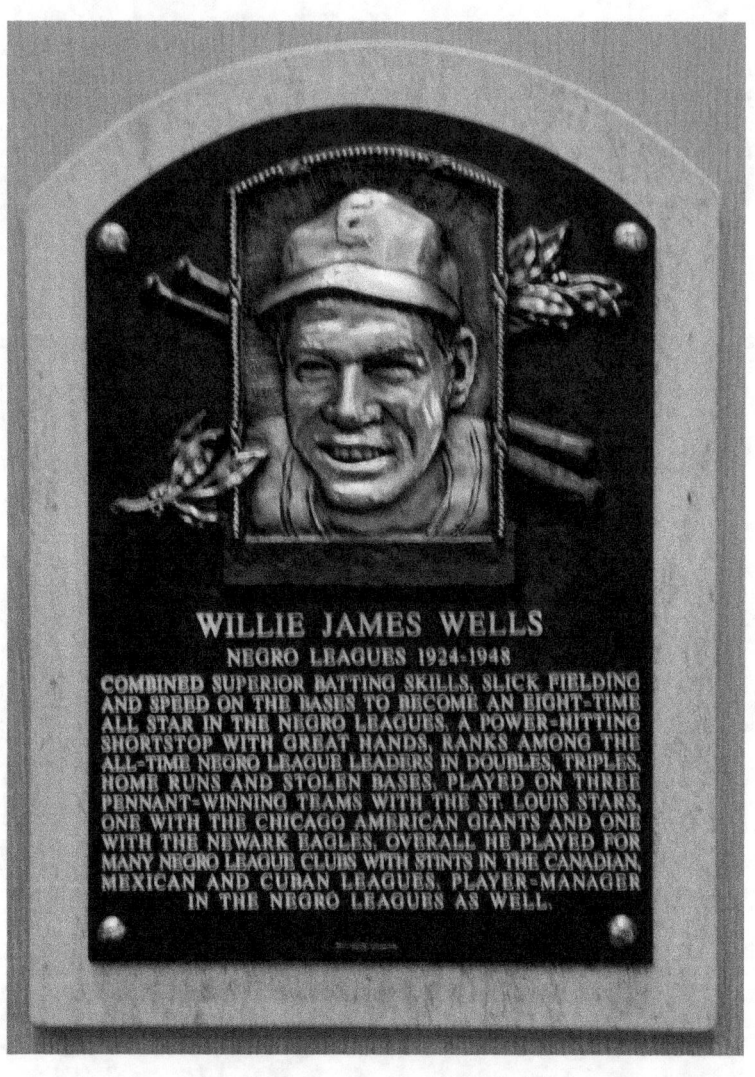

Sportswriters had a difficult time coming up with enough superlatives to describe shortstop Willie Wells. He was a rare shortstop who combined fielding excellence with power hitting. He starred in both the Negro and Latin American Leagues. Mexican fans were the ones who gave him the nickname "The Devil" because of his excellent fielding at shortstop. Opponents would comment, "Don't hit the ball to shortstop, the Devil is there." In fact, Monte Irvin commented that Wells was the best shortstop he ever saw. Black baseball historian Ric Roberts agreed with Irvin, saying, " I have watched him over ten years and never saw him make an error."

When Wells played the infield for the Newark Eagles, that infield was called "the million-dollar infield" consisting of Wells, Suttles & Dandridge, all eventually inductees into the Baseball Hall of Fame.

Wells was a consistent 300 hitter in the Negro League. He would often lead the league in homeruns. Buck O'Neil, in the game over 70 years said, "Wells could hit to all fields, hit with power, bunt and stretch a single into a double and a double into a triple.

It has been said, "As great a ball player as Ozzie Smith was with the St. Louis Cardinals, old-timers who saw Willie Wells play for the St. Louis Stars still haven't seen his equal." According to Cowan "Bubba" Hyde, Wells hit 25 – 30 home runs a year and he hit .325 or .330 every year. He was one of the smartest players ever to play in the Negro League.

On September 10, 1933, the East-West game was inaugurated before a rain-soaked crowd of 20,000. Fans attending the first black summer classic saw seven future Hall of Famers take the field: Willie Wells, Cool Papa Bell, Bill Foster, Oscar Charleston, Josh Gibson, Judy Johnson and Turkey Stearnes. Over the next 20 seasons the East-West All-Star Game ranked amongst black America's favorite sporting events. From 1933 to 1950 the Classic attracted tens of thousand fans each season. Games were held in Comiskey Park, Chicago, Yankee Stadium, New York City, Griffith Stadium, Washington, D.C. and Municipal Stadium,

Cleveland, Ohio. Sometimes they held a second All-Star Game, that's how popular it became not only in the black community but in the white community as well.

Even though Wells never made it to the major leagues, Wells is given credit for helping the next generation of players, such as Jackie Robinson, Don Newcombe, Joe Black and Ernie Banks. He would tell these guys, "Watch yourself. You never know who's looking to sign you."

Willie Wells was the Manager of the Newark Eagles (1942 & 1945) and the Indianapolis Clowns (1947).

He is known for being the first player to wear a protective helmet after he was beaned in 1942. While playing for the Newark Eagles, Wells was knocked unconscious by one of Bill Byrd's spitballs. Even though the doctor told him to sit out a few days, he came back the next day wearing a construction worker's helmet while he batted.

Wells' Lifetime Stats:

Games played:	756
At bats:	2824
Batting Average:	.320
Hits:	905
Homeruns:	100
Triples:	47
Doubles:	166
Runs scored:	629
Walks:	368
Stolen bases:	119

16

"BULLET" JOE ROGAN

BORN: CHARLES WILBER ROGAN on July 28, 1893
in Oklahoma City, Oklahoma
DIED: March 4, 1967 in Kansas City, Missouri
NICKNAME: "Bullet"
Inducted into the Baseball Hall of Fame in 1998

Rogan began playing baseball at the age of 30, when he played with the Kansas City Monarchs. He remained with the Monarchs for eleven years. His pitching form was beautiful. He had a perfect wind-up and became a premier pitcher in the Negro Leagues. He eventually held the record for the most strikeouts in a single season. He had a great curveball and fastball.

Rogan joined the Army in 1911 and remained enlisted until 1915, when he returned to civilian life. His first game back, pitching for the Monarchs, he threw a 1-hitter against the American Giants.

Casey Stengel, Yankee manager marveled, "Rogan is one of the best - if not the best - pitchers that ever pitched in the Negro League."

. . .

Rogan was also a great hitter. From 1922-30 while playing for the Monarchs, Rogan's batting average was over .300 every year. He was often the clean-up hitter. In all, he compiled a .338 batting average which was 10th best among all Negro Leaguers. Rogan also showed tremendous hitting prowess while playing against white teams. In 25 games against major league teams, Rogan batted .329.

In 1924, with Rogan on the mound, the Kansas City Monarchs beat the Hilldale Athletic Club in the first Black World Series.

J. L. Wilkinson, the owner of the Monarchs, saw the potential of Rogan and asked him to become a player/manager, which Rogan gladly accepted. In 1929, the Monarchs, with Rogan as manager, won the Negro National League pennant. As the manager, Rogan was a great teacher in all aspects of the game. He taught the younger players the tools to become better players in the art of hitting - especially bunting, hitting and running.

From 1920 to 1930, Rogan averaged 30 games a year on the mound and, according to J.L. Wilkinson, was never once relieved. The nickname "Bullet" came about because of his great fastball. Toward the end of his career, he was sometimes called Bullet Joe.

After his retirement from the playing field, Rogan returned home and had a civil-service job in Kansas City. He also umpired in the Negro League games for several years before he passed away in 1967.

• • •

In 1930, J.L. Wilkinson, who owned a traveling lighting set, had the Monarchs play in the first night baseball game in the Negro League. Because of this lighting set, the fans were enthusiastic to see the game. There were approximately 3000 fans in attendance.

Rogan retired in 1938, and his lifetime batting average was .338, placing him 4th in the Negro League.

Rogan's Lifetime Pitching stats:
Games Started:	153
Games Completed:	128
Shutouts:	15
Innings Pitched:	1454
Wins:	119
Losses:	50
Strikeouts:	882
Walks:	364
ERA:	3.68

Rogan's Player stats:
Batting Average:	.338
Hits:	1292
Runs Scored:	595

17

SMOKEY JOE WILLIAMS

BORN: *JOE WILLIAMS on April 6, 1886 at Seguin, Texas*
DIED: *February 25, 1951 at New York City*
Nickname: *"Smokey" and "Cyclone Joe"*
Inducted into the National Baseball Hall of Fame in 1999.

Smokey Joe Williams was often mentioned as black baseball's greatest pitcher, considered by many to be superior to Cannonball Redding, Bill Foster, Frick Wickware, and even Satchel Paige. A 1952 poll of Negro baseball insiders by the *Pittsburgh Courier* gave Williams the nod over Paige by a 20 to 19 vote as the best of all time. Many have opined that during the first half of the Negro League years, Williams was what Paige was in the second half—the best pitcher in the game.

At the start of Williams' first season with the Chicago Leland Giants, Frank Leland, the team's owner, alerted the fans about what to expect from their new right-hander. He suggested, "If you have ever witnessed the speed of a pebble in a storm, you have not even seen the speed possessed by this wonderful Texan Giant. He is the king of all pitchers hailing from the Lone Star State."

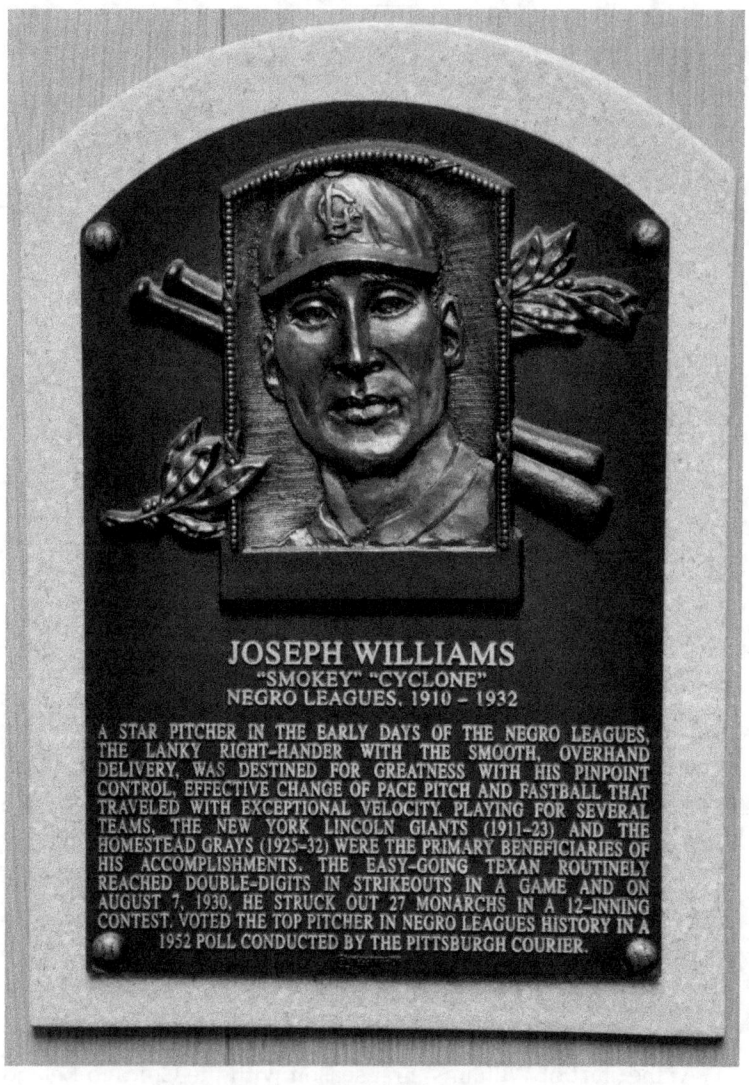

Baseball historian Jim Riley points out three performances

against major league clubs that showcased the exceptional talent Williams possessed. In 1912, Williams shut out the world champion New York Giants, 6-0. In a 1915 matchup against a major league club, he outpitched Grover Cleveland Alexander when he struck out ten batters and pitched a three-hit shutout to beat the Philadelphia Phillies 1-0. In a third showcase performance, in 1917, he pitched a no-hitter and struck out twenty batters against the New York Giants. He lost the game 1-0 on an error.

Williams won two out of three games against Satchel Paige while pitching for the Homestead Grays. Smokey Joe was involved in many pitching duels during his storied career in the Negro League, but one game speaks volumes about his excellent pitching.

On August 7, 1930 he was involved in a titanic struggle against the Kansas City Monarchs' ace Chet Brewer. Playing under a primitive lighting system at the time, the two pitchers battled for 12 innings. Brewer was known for his cut balls, which he roughed up with an emery board. He struck out 19 men. In retaliation, Williams spat tobacco juice on the ball, making it almost impossible to see. At the ripe old age of 45, he struck out 25 batters that night. The game ended only after the Grays' Oscar Charleston walked and Chaney White followed with a ground ball that smacked off third base, scoring Charleston when nobody could see where the ball went.

Two sportswriters, Sid Mercer and Bozeman Butler, believed, "Williams was the best pitcher with Major League Stars." Butler rated Williams on par with Christy Mathewson, who happened to be Butler's best friend.

<u>Williams' lifetime stats</u>:

Games Started:	256
Games Completed:	209
Innings Pitched:	1760
Runs Allowed:	475
Wins:	156
Losses:	94
Strikeouts:	1571
Walks:	568
ERA:	2.45

18

TURKEY STEARNES

BORN: NORMAN THOMAS STEARNES on May 8,
  1901 at Nashville, Tennessee
DIED: September 4, 1979 at Detroit, Michigan
NICKNAME: "Turkey"
Inducted in the National Baseball Hall of Fame in 2000

Turkey Stearnes learned the art of pitching while in high school. He threw and batted left-handed, and because of his ability to hit, was soon developed into an outfielder. His first year of professional baseball was as an outfielder for the Nashville Grays. He then went to the Negro League as an outfielder for the Montgomery Gray Sox.

In 1922 while playing for the Gray Sox, he was scouted and signed by the Detroit Stars for the 1923 season. In his first game with the Detroit Stars in 1923 he hit for the cycle. He followed that with games where he hit three triples and multiple home runs. That year he hit .366 with 18 home runs and 89 runs batted in. His on base percentage (OBP) was .403, and he had a remarkable .723 slugging percentage. Stearnes played for the Stars until 1930, when he was traded in mid-season to the New York Lincoln Giants. He was traded back to the Stars in 1931, and played for them again in 1937.

Jimmy Cruthsfield, one of Turkey's teammates, said, "You would never think Stearnes would hit a ball far. He had a weird stance and looked like he was going to fall over." One story about Stearnes' power is well known. Bojangles Robinson came to watch a game when Stearnes was playing for the Los Angeles White Sox during winter ball. Bojangles offered five dollars to anyone who hit a home run. Turkey hit four that game. Bojangles commented, "It's time for me to stop handing out money." Mr. Robinson should have expected that the extra expense would be added to his ticket price. After all, Turkey Stearnes won seven home run titles in the Negro Leagues.

Historian Lesley A. Heaphy wrote, "Stearnes was a leadoff batter even though he had power. His speed and high average made him a great choice to be on the top of the order. He had great speed along with great arm strength."

Buck O'Neil commented, "Stearnes was quirky with his bats. He carried them in a special case which looked like a musical instrument case. One day, while on the road, I knocked on Stearnes hotel room door, and when I entered the room, there was Stearnes sitting on the bed in his pajamas talking to his bats."

Stearnes played one season of winter ball in Cuba. He then opted to play winter ball for nine years in the California Winter League for St. Louis, hitting over .300 in each season.

In 1931 while playing for the Nashville Elite Giants, Stearnes led the league in batting (.377), base hits (48) and home runs (8).

In 1938 Stearnes decided to retire from baseball and went back home to work, but in 1964 at age 44 he once again decided to play baseball. He joined the Toledo Cubs in the newly formed United States Negro League as their field captain.

Satchel Paige and Cool Papa Bell both observed, "Turkey had a weird batter's stance but he hit the ball to all fields and often out of the park. He was as good a hitter as Josh Gibson."

<u>Stearnes' Lifetime Stats</u>:

At Bats:	3370
Batting Average:	.351
Hits:	1356
Home Runs:	202
Triples:	127
Doubles:	224
Walks:	324
Stolen Bases:	143

19

HILTON SMITH

*BORN: HILTON LEE SMITH on February 27, 1907 in
Giddings, Texas
DIED: November 18, 1983 in Kansas City, Missouri
Inducted into the National Baseball Hall of Fame
in 2001*

Hilton Smith came from a small town, Giddings, Texas. His father, a teacher, regarded education highly and sent Hilton to Prairie View A&M, encouraging him to pursue his dream of becoming a professional baseball player. Hilton stayed for two years and pitched on the baseball team.

His father continued to encourage Hilton to pursue his dream of playing professional baseball. During this time, the Depression was in full swing when Hilton finally entered professional baseball, and he was happy to have a job playing.

• • •

Hilton joined the Austin Black Senators in 1931. The Austin team was a farm team in the Negro Leagues. Hilton won a game 4-3 against the Chicago American Giants. Soon people noticed Hilton's talent, and he was eventually signed to play in the Southern Negro League with the Monroe (Louisiana) Monarchs in 1932. He remained with the Monarchs until 1935.

Hilton then joined the Kansas City Monarchs in 1936. On the team was Satchel Paige. People felt Hilton was equal in talent with Paige, but he often went unnoticed. That is how he became known as "Invisible Man." Smith was known as Paige's "caddy" because Smith would come into a game to pitch the last six innings after Paige pitched the first three. Everyone knowledgeable of the game still considered Hilton Smith as the "Money Pitcher."

Hilton Smith reminisced, "I won 161 games and lost 32, but most people do not know me. I took my baseball seriously. Doing the job and being the best pitcher was my aim. I'm taking nothing away from Satch. He produced and could clown around and get away with it. Being in his shadow really hurt me, but I couldn't do nothing about it. My personality was completely different from Satch. I never did crawl out from under his shadow."

The highlight of Smith's career came in 1937 when he pitched a perfect game for the Kansas City Monarchs against the Chicago American Giants.

Smith won more than 20 games in each of his dozen seasons with the Kansas City Monarchs, which included a record 25 victories and only two defeats in 1941. From 1939-1942, Smith posted season records of 25-2, 21-3, 25-1 and 22-5.

Buck O'Neil commented, "Smith was the best pitcher from 1940-46. Even Johnny Mize and Stan Musial couldn't believe the great curveball he had. He would have been a great pitcher in the Major Leagues." Hall of Famer Bob Feller also thought,

"Smith played in the shadow of Satchel Paige, but he was a better pitcher than Paige. Smith had the greatest curveball in the Negro League." While barnstorming against major league teams, Smith had a record of 6 wins and 1 loss.

In the *New Historical Baseball Abstract,* Bill James called Hilton Smith the best Negro league player in 1939, 1941 and 1942. In James' opinion, Satchel Paige only earned that honor once in 1936.

Hilton Smith and Jackie Robinson served together in the United States Army. Although Robinson was able to play on the Army football team with white players, he and Smith were not permitted to play on the Army baseball team with white players.

When Hilton Smith was discharged from the Army, the Brooklyn Dodgers offered him a minor league contract with their farm team. Smith turned the offer down, refusing to sign, saying, "The Dodgers are decades too late. Besides, I would have been paid less."

What most people want out of life is to be worth something and to feel important to someone. To be recognized by your peers is desirable. His peers and others praised Hilton Smith. People sometimes only remember those who have great bravado.

Hilton was finally recognized by his peers and inducted into the Baseball Hall of Fame in 2001.

. . .

Descartes once said, "You cannot prove the existence of another, you can only prove your own existence." Hilton Smith proved this.

Smith's Lifetime Stats:

Games Started:	67
Games Completed:	40
Innings Pitched:	672
Perfect Games:	1
Wins:	72
Losses:	25
Strikeouts:	398
Hits:	565
Runs:	257
Walks:	79

20

RAY BROWN

BORN: RAYMOND BROWN on February 23, 1908 at
Ashland Grove, Ohio
DIED: February 8, 1965 at Dayton, Ohio
Inducted into the Baseball Hall of Fame in 2006.

Ray Brown played for the Homestead Grays from 1932-1945. In 1933, the owner of the Grays, Cum Posey, was having financial trouble which made him afraid of losing the Homestead Grays. He approached Sonny Jackson, a local numbers man, to invest in the Grays. Jackson agreed, under the condition he was named President and Treasurer of the team. Posey agreed to these terms as long as he was in control of the field operations of the Grays. In 1933, Gus Greenlee, owner of the Pittsburgh Crawfords, raided the Grays and convinced players to play for the Crawfords. Posey was able to hold on to Smokey Joe Williams and Ray Brown, and with the arrival of Buck Leonard, in 1935, the Grays joined the Negro National League and were a .500 ball club.

Ray Brown was an exceptional pitcher for the Grays, helping them win eight out of nine pennants in 1932-1945. Ray Brown was noted for a great curveball as well as an accurate fastball. He was selected twice to play in the East-West All-Star Classic.

Brown led the Negro National League (NNL) in wins in 1939, 1941 and 1942. He is ranked among the all-time pitching leaders in Negro League history. Historian Jim Riley captures

Brown's formidable pitching presence well. "The Homestead Grays ace had a sinker, slider and a fine fastball, but his curveball was his bread and butter pitch. Later in his career he developed an effective knuckleball and had great control of all his pitches."

In 1944 Brown pitched for Homestead Grays against the Birmingham Black Barons in the Negro League World Series. He pitched a one-hitter, but his best season was in 1940, when his record was 15-4, with an ERA of 2.61. He won twenty-eight (28) consecutive games in the 1936-37 season.

Brown played five seasons of Winter Ball in Cuba. His statistics there were: a win-loss record of 46-20, 57 complete games, and an ERA of 2.45. Brown also played Winter Ball in Puerto Rico and Mexico in 1939 and 1940, and his combined record was: 51-36 with an ERA of 3.31.

Ray Brown's Lifetime stats:

Games Started:	126
Games Completed:	106
Shutouts:	13
Innings Pitched:	1150
Runs Allowed:	529
Wins:	92
Losses:	41
Strikeouts:	449
Hits:	1115
Walks:	225
ERA:	4.14

WILLARD BROWN

BORN: WILLARD JESSIE BROWN on June 26, 1915
   at Shreveport, Louisiana
DIED: August 4, 1996 at Houston, Texas
Nickname: "El Hombre" & "Home-Run"
Inducted into the Baseball Hall of Fame in 2006

Brown was given the nickname of "El Hombre," meaning, "That Man." He played Winter ball in Puerto Rico in 1947-48 and 1949-50. Both years he won the Triple Crown. Prior to playing in Puerto Rico, Brown played Winter ball in Cuba in 1937-1938.

Brown began playing professional baseball in 1934 when he joined the Monroe Monarchs of the Southern Negro League. In 1936 he was signed by the Kansas City Monarchs of the Negro National League.

Brown & Dodger Jerseys

Josh Gibson referred to Brown as "Home Run Brown," as he hit many home runs when he played for the Kansas City Monarchs. Brown played for the Kansas City Monarchs from 1936-1942 and again in 1945 when he returned from the military in Europe during World War Two. Brown helped the Monarchs win the Negro National League Championship in 1946. He played in eight East-West All-Star Games, the first in 1936.

In July 1947 Brown was signed by the St Louis Browns half way through the season. He became the first Black ballplayer to hit a home run in the American League—a pinch hit, inside-the-parker off Hal Newhouser, but the St. Louis Browns released him after a month.

Brown returned to Puerto Rico to play Winter Ball for the 1947-1948 season. He had a .432 BA, 27 HRs and 16 RBIs. With those statistics, Brown won the Triple Crown. Brown admitted, "I enjoyed playing in Puerto Rico because the people treated me much better than the people in the United States." On the same team with Brown in Puerto Rico was Elston Howard, who eventually was the first black player signed to play with the New York Yankees.

Brown was black baseball's premier home-run hitter of the 1940's; he was characterized by Jim Riley as a "bundle of unlimited and largely unfulfilled potential." But given the talent of Brown, one would have to agree with Jim Riley's assessment. Riley further stated, "Willard Brown was a slugger who was exceptionally fast in the field, a good base runner, and an excellent gloveman with a great arm. Noted as a big-game player, he was at his best in front of a large crowd."

Willard Brown retired from baseball in 1958. He went on to live in Houston, Texas.

Brown's Lifetime stats:
At bats:	901
Batting Average:	.337
Hits:	304
Home Runs:	30
Triples:	25
Doubles:	42
Runs scored:	172
Run Batted In:	139

22

ANDY COOPER

BORN: *ANDREW LEWIS COOPER on March 4,*
1896 in Waco, Texas
DIED: *June 10, 1941 in Waco, Texas*
NICKNAMES: *"Lefty" & "Andy"*
Inducted into the Baseball Hall of Fame in 2006

Cooper was an excellent pitcher in the Negro League, pitching for the Detroit Stars and Kansas City Monarchs. He had excellent control, mixed his pitches and changed speeds. He also had an excellent fastball.

Negro League historian Dick Clark once said of Cooper. "In my estimation, the greatest black pitcher ever to pitch for Detroit that's for the Stars or the Tigers."

While Cooper was pitching for Kansas City Monarchs in 1929, they were the Negro National League Champs. Cooper's records while pitching for them in 1928 and 1929 was 13-7 and 13-3. In

1936, which was his best year with the Monarchs, Cooper's record was 27-8.

Cooper was equally effective when he pitched for the Detroit Stars from the years 1922-1927. His record in those years was 14-5, 15-8, 12-5, 12-8 and 17-8.

. . .

In 1930, Cooper decided to barnstorm with other Negro League players. They went to the Orient to play Winter Ball, and played in Japan, China and the Philippines. Cooper remembered, "In every country they were fantastic fans, who appreciated us playing. No matter wherever we went they treated us with kindness and respect in every country we played."

The Kansas City Monarchs, in 1937, won the first pennant in the newly formed Negro American League. Cooper was the winning pitcher. He eventually became the manager of the Monarchs. He pitched a no-hitter in his forties. Cooper was a great teacher of the game for the younger players on the team. O'Neil said he was the best manager he ever played for. He was a father figure who helped all the players. He was a stern when he had to be, but he was easy to be around. Andy would comment to the players, "You know curfew is at midnight, and I know you guys know this. So I know you're gonna be in by midnight." Other managers would sort of threaten their players in order to get them to follow the rules of curfew. Guys on the team would feel guilty to not abide by the midnight curfew as they felt they were violating the trust of Andy.

According to a scouting report prepared by famed Negro League player and manager Buck O'Neil, Cooper had a live arm with a total command of all his pitches, which included a running fastball, tight curveball and a biting screwball.

Russ J. Cowans, a reporter for *The Chicago Defender*, wrote, "Cooper could almost put the ball any place he wanted it to go. In addition, Cooper had a keen sense of the batters. He knew the weakness of every batter in the league."

<u>Cooper's Lifetime stats</u>:

Games Started:	162
Games Completed:	99
Shutouts:	14
No-Hitters:	1
Innings Pitched:	1592
Wins:	116
Losses:	57
Strikeouts:	578
Walks:	244
Hits Surrendered:	1564

23

FRANK GRANT

BORN: ULYSSES FRANKLIN GRANT on August 1,
   1865 in Pittsfield, Massachusetts
DIED: May 27, 1937 in New York City, New York
NICKNAME: "Frank"
Inducted into the National Baseball Hall of Fame
   in 2006

"Frank" Grant was one of the best fielding second baseman in the Negro League. He was also a great hitter. He batted and threw right-handed.

In 1886, at the age of 21, Grant became a professional baseball player, playing for Meriden (CT) of the Eastern League. After the Meriden team disbanded, Grant joined the Buffalo Bisons of the International League late in the season. Grant played second base and batted .344 in 49 games. He also pitched on occasion.

Grant was back with the Bisons in the International League in 1887. The team and league were ripe with racial tension. Some of the white players refused to take the team photo during Spring Training if Grant was included. Only after discussions between the players and the manager did they agree to appear in the photo.

· · ·

There were also numerous racial incidents. At a game in Toronto on July 27, 1887 when Grant came to bat, some of the fans began chanting, "Kill the N ------." Grant began wearing wooden shin guards to protect his legs because white players would try to injure him while sliding into second base. Even the umpires acted in a discriminatory manner, making incorrect calls against the black players. Despite the hostile atmosphere, Grant excelled in 1887. He batted .353, stole 40 bases and led the league in home runs with 11 while playing in 105 games. The racially charged atmosphere was so great that International League officials banned further signings of Black players by the teams in the middle of the season. Black players already under contract, including Grant, were allowed to continue playing. In 1889, the Jim Crow Laws prohibited Black ballplayers from playing in white leagues.

In 1889 Grant left the Bisons and joined the Cuban Giants of the Negro League. On August 17, 1889, at Olympic Park, Grant had a terrific game. He drove in eight runs by hitting a grand slam, a two-run homer, a two-run triple, and a single.

He then barnstormed in upper New York when he joined a new club, the Colored All-Americans. He played in 67 games batting, .313.

Grant's last year was 1903 when he played for the Philadelphia Giants.

<u>Grant's Lifetime Stats</u>:

At Bats:	1115
Batting Average:	.345
Hits:	388
Home Runs:	19
Triples:	22
Doubles:	74
Runs Scored:	255

PETE HILL

BORN: JOHN PRESTON HILL on November 12, 1882
at Buena, Virginia
DIED: December 19, 1951 at Buffalo, New York
Nickname: "Pete"
Inducted into the Hall of Fame in 2006

Some baseball historians have stated, "Pete Hill was the first great outfielder in black baseball." He could hit both lefthanders and righthanders equally well, and became the backbone of the great Chicago American Giants teams for Rube Foster.

Hill played for several famed independent African-American teams - the Philadelphia Giants (1904-07), Leland Giants (1908-10) and Chicago American Giants (1911-18).

Cum Posey, the owner of the Homestead Grays, reminisced, "Hill was the most consistent hitter in his lifetime; besides, he was a feared line-drive hitter." Hill was a consistently steady hitter for the years 1910, 1911, 1912 and 1913. In those years his batting average was .413, .400, .357 and .302. His total average for those four years was .371.

In 1908, Pete Hill went to play in the Cuban Winter League where he batted .343. He led the league in hitting in 1911, with a batting average of .365. In 1917, he batted .371.

. . .

Ben Taylor, a magnificent hitter himself, had this to say about Pete Hill: "The time was he was numbered among the greatest in the game, and there will probably never be an equal as a hitter. I think he is the most dangerous hitter in a pinch in baseball."

In 1921 Pete Hill played for the Detroit Stars, where he batted .391. Baseball historian Jim Reilly suggested, "If there was an all-star team picked during the Dead Ball Era, Pete Hill would be flanked in the outfield by Ty Cobb and Tris Speaker."

Pete Hill became a manager of the Chicago American Giants, Detroit Stars and later the Baltimore Black Sox. Hill credited his managing skills to Rube Foster, while Foster was manager of the Detroit Stars and Hill played for them.

Lawrence D. Hogan's book, *Shades of Glory: The Negro Leagues and the Story of African-American Baseball*, describes Hill as a "restless type, always in motion, jumping back and forth trying to draw a throw from the pitcher."

Pete Hill's great-nephew, Ron Hill said, "A lot of people forget about the baseball players who were pioneers of the game. They're forgotten like they never existed, but they are a part of American history. How can you talk about baseball without talking about Pete Hill?"

In 1927 Pete Hill retired from baseball. He returned to Buffalo and worked steady on the railroad.

Pete Hill's Lifetime stats:

Games Played:	446
At Bats:	2206
Batting Average:	.297
Hits:	656
Home Runs:	36
Triples:	49
Doubles:	84
Runs Scored:	438
Runs Batted In:	281
Walks:	285
Stolen Bases:	114

25

BIZ MACKEY

BORN: JAMES RALEIGH MACKEY on July 27, 1897
  in Eagle Pass, Texas
DIED: September 22, 1965 in Los Angeles, California
NICKNAME: "BIZ"
Inducted into the Baseball Hall of Fame in 2006

Biz Mackey was one of six children. Some records indicate he was born in Eagle Pass, Texas while other records indicate it was Caldwell County. His parents were farmers.

Mackey married Ora Lee Dorn at a very young age, and they had four children, a girl (Narcissus) and three boys. His grandson, Riley Mackey Odoms, had a long career with the Denver Broncos. They took up residence in Luling, Texas.

• • •

Eventually Mackey, Ora and their children moved to Dallas, where he played baseball and was a laborer in 1918. He then took a job in a railroad warehouse.

At the time, Mackey was only 16 years old. He joined his brothers Ernest and Ray playing for the Luling Oilers, a local semi-pro team. Mackey played as a catcher and pitcher.

. . .

Records could be incorrect or lost, but some sources state in 1918 Mackey played for the San Antonio Black Aces while others say he played for the Dallas Black Giants. One thing is certain, he played for 30 years, playing for many teams in the Negro League - the Hilldale Giants, Philadelphia Stars, Newark Eagles, Indianapolis ABC's and the Baltimore/Washington Elite Giants. Wherever he played, he was a proven leader behind the plate and, later in his career, as a great manager.

While playing for the Hilldale Giants, Biz Mackey won the batting title in 1931 with an average of .359. He was also chosen to play in five East-West All-Star Classics.

Most players didn't receive the best salaries while playing in the Negro League, therefore many went to play Winter Ball in other countries. Mackey played Winter Ball in Japan. He observed, "The people in Japan treated me and the other players great, better than we were treated at home in the United States."

Mackey enjoyed playing in Japan. He returned there in 1927, 1934 and 1935.

Biz Mackey decided to become the manager of the Newark Eagles during the 1940-41 season and returned to manage them again during the 1946-47 season. Both seasons the Eagles had winning records. Mackey was responsible for mentoring Monte Irvin, Larry Doby, Don Newcomb and Roy Campanella, who all became Major Leaguers and eventual Hall of Famers. While he managed the Eagles, they beat the Kansas City Monarchs to win the Negro League World Series. Pitching on the Monarchs was Satchel Paige.

• • •

Mackey also managed the Baltimore Elite Giants in 1937. On that team was 15-year-old Roy Campanella. Campanella admitted, "Mackey taught me how to become a major league catcher."

Biz Mackey decided to retire after the 1950-51 season. He moved back to Los Angeles and began working as a forklift operator. In 1952, he was selected by the *Pittsburgh Courier* poll as the Negro League's greatest catcher, ahead of Josh Gibson. Mackey received more accolades on May 7, 1959, when Roy Campanella was honored at the Los Angeles Memorial Coliseum following his paralysis from a car accident. Mackey was introduced to the crowd of over 93,000 for the exhibition game between the Dodgers and New York Yankees.

Mackey lived in Los Angeles until his death in 1965.

Mackey's Lifetime Stats:

At Bats:	2997
Batting Average:	.328
Hits:	982
Home Runs:	48
Triples:	42
Doubles:	135
Runs Scored:	467

26

EFFA MANLEY

BORN: *EFFA LOUISE MANLEY on March 27, 1897 in Philadelphia, Pennsylvania*
DIED: *April 16, 1981 in Los Angeles, California*
Inducted into the National Baseball Hall of Fame in 2006.

*E*ffa Manley co-owned the Newark Eagles with her husband, Abe Manley.

After completing high school, Effa moved to New York City in 1916, where she resided in Harlem. She found a job in Manhattan, working in a millinery shop.

In 1932, Effa Manley had a major change in her life. She was a huge baseball fan, rooting for Babe Ruth and the New York Yankees. While she was at the 1932 World Series at Yankee Stadium, she met Abe Manley. They were married in 1933.

In 1934, the Negro National League owners awarded Abe a franchise, the Brooklyn Eagles. The team played their home games in Ebbets Field, which was the home of the Brooklyn Dodgers. Some of the players on the Eagles were Leon Day, Rap Dixon, and Ted "Double Duty" Radcliffe.

Abe may have owned the Eagles, but Effa Manley would soon oversee the management of the team.

. . .

In 1936, the Manleys purchased the Newark Dodgers and combined them with the Brooklyn Eagles. The Manleys relocated the team to Ruppert Stadium in Newark, New Jersey.

The Manleys were instrumental in working to improve the management of the Negro National League. Abe Manley was elected to be Vice-President, and in 1938 he was also elected Treasurer.

Soon thereafter, Effa Manley began to arrange the Eagles' schedules, book the accommodations for the players on the road, purchase equipment, and negotiate contracts for the team. She was a strict disciplinarian, and kept her eyes on the behavior of the players. Pitcher James Walker noted, "Mrs. Manley was very strict with the players. She would call you into her office, tell you how to dress on the road, who to associate with. But when you had a personal problem, you went to Mrs. Manley. She was very understanding, as long as you toed the line."

Effa Manley was very active in Civil Rights issues. She would question employers as to why they refused to hire blacks. She was eventually elected as the Treasurer of the New Jersey N.A.A.C.P.

In 1946, the Newark Eagles, after sporting a regular season record of 53 wins, 24 losses and 3 ties, beat the Kansas City Monarchs in a seven game series to become champions of the Negro League. At that time the team had four future Hall of Fame players on the roster - Leon Day, Larry Doby, Monte Irvin, and Biz Mackey.

. . .

Three more future Hall of Fame players joined the Eagles from 1935 - 1948. They were Ray Dandridge, Mule Suttles, and Willie Wells.

Abe Manley died in 1952.

Effa Manley moved to California after her second marriage failed. She remained active in baseball and the integration of more Negro players into the Major Leagues. She wrote a letter to LA Dodger owner Walter O'Malley expressing her thoughts on signing players to the Dodgers. She never received an answer. Effa Manley continued to preserve the history of the Negro League.

In 1971, the National Baseball Hall of Fame created a special committee to elect players from the Negro League. Prior to disbanding in 1977, the Committee elected nine players into the Hall of Fame. Effa continued to fight for the players. She complained that those inducted should have plaques with their names on them, just like the white inductees. It was finally done.

In 1976 Effa co-wrote a book with Leon Herbert Hardwick, entitled, *Negro Baseball......Before Integration*. This was one of the first publications about Negro League baseball.

In 2006, the Hall of Fame Committee once again convened and elected 17 new black players from the Negro League into the National Baseball Hall Of Fame. Also elected was Effa Manley, who became the first female inducted into the Hall of Fame.

. . .

Effa Manley died on April 16, 1981. "She loved baseball" is inscribed on her tombstone.

27

JOSE MENDEZ

BORN: JOSE MENDEZ on March 19, 1888 in
   Cardenas, Cuba
DIED: November 6, 1928 in Havana, Cuba
Nickname: "El Diamante Negro" (The Black Diamond)
Inducted into the National Baseball Hall of Fame in
   2006

Mendez was a terrific shortstop and a great pitcher with a strong arm. Turmoil during the years Mendez played in Cuba resulted in poor record-keeping and lost records. Because of this, many people felt Mendez was selected for induction into the National Baseball Hall of Fame on a sympathy vote. A closer look at his impact on the game shows that is not true.

In 1909, *Sporting Life* reported that Mendez was coming to pitch in the United States. After seeing Mendez pitch in Cuba, New York Giants owner John McGraw was convinced of his talents. McGraw told a sportswriter that he'd pay $50,000 for Mendez's release from Almendares.

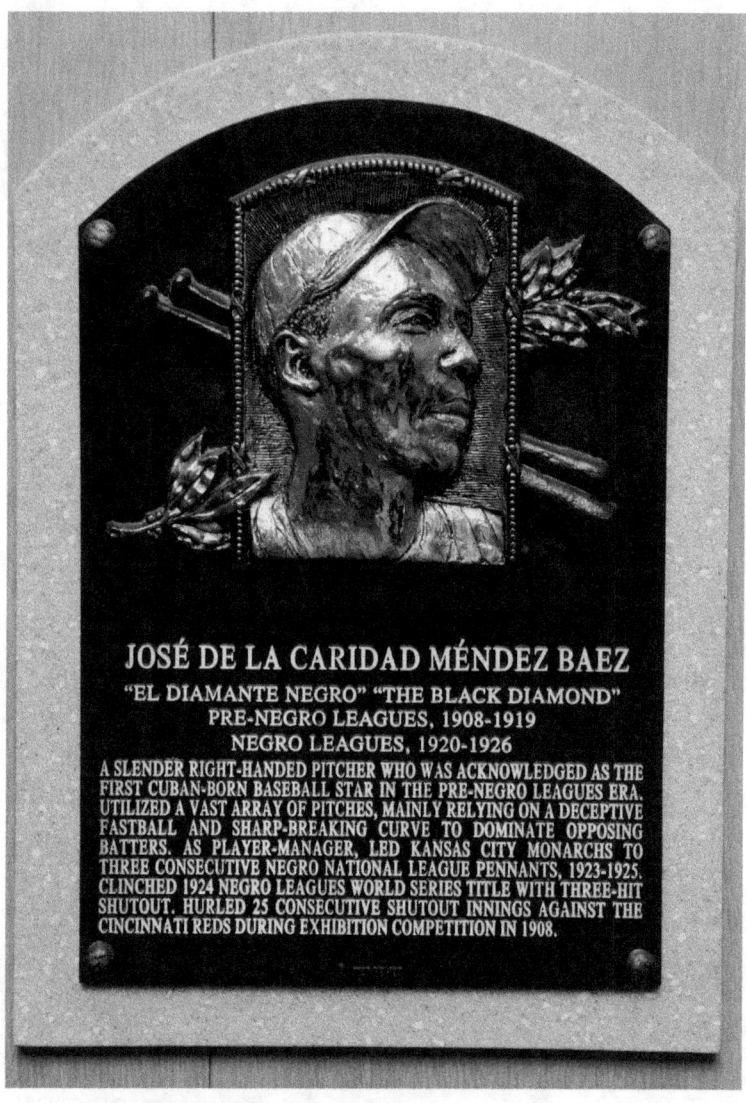

Mendez's assortment of pitches became a source of misery for the Major Leaguers. Twice in his career Mendez compiled a scoreless streak of 25 innings against one team - pitching against the Cincinnati Reds in 1908 and the Detroit Tigers in 1909. In a 1909 game, he held Cincinnati hitless through nine innings before settling on a one-hit shutout victory.

In 1920, Mendez became player/manager of the Kansas City Monarchs. In 1923, Mendez's record was 15-5 with a 1.89 ERA, the best in the North American Negro League.

The first Negro World Series was played in Chicago between the Hilldale Daisies and Mendez's Kansas City Monarchs. It was a ten game series. In the first nine games, each team won four games and one game ended in a tie. The deciding game was played on Monday, October 20, 1924.

The starting pitcher for the Monarchs wasn't decided until game time. Many thought that Mendez would not be pitching, since his doctor had told him that he should not pitch due to an operation he had had on his injured arm. The doctor told him that if he did pitch he might cause permanent damage to the arm. Mendez told his doctor, "I don't care. I am going to pitch as I want to win this game." Mendez pitched one of the most memorable games in the history of America's national game.

For seven innings both pitchers dominated. "Script" Lee, the Hilldale pitcher, befuddled the Monarchs with his submarine pitching style. In the eighth inning, Lee suddenly, inexplicably, changed, and began to throw overhand. The Monarchs began to hit Lee, and finally broke through. They scored five runs that inning. They won the game 5–0, making Jose Mendez the winning pitcher. In the series, Mendez had a 1.42 ERA.

• • •

Jose Mendez was inducted into the Cuban Hall Of Fame in 1939.

<u>Mendez Lifetime Pitching Stats</u>:

Games Started:	91
Games Completed:	66
Innings Pitched:	1315
Wins:	95
Losses:	46
Strikeouts:	725
Walks:	332
ERA:	3.32
Shutouts:	19

<u>Mendez Lifetime Player Stats</u>:

Games Played:	124
At Bats:	2480
Hits:	728
Home Runs:	3
Triples:	30
Doubles:	79
Runs Scored:	328

28

ALEX POMPEZ

BORN: ALEJANDRO POMPEZ on May 3, 1890 in
  Key West, Florida
DIED: March 14, 1974 in Flushing, New York
NICKNAME: "Alex"
Inducted into the Baseball Hall of Fame in 2006

*A*lex Pompez was among the most influential owners in black baseball history. His New York Cuban Stars were a top team for more than thirty years. Pompez was specifically influential in bringing together the Negro League and Caribbean League so that players from both leagues could play against each other.

Pompez was the owner of the Dyckman Oval Ballpark in Manhattan. When he bought the park, he renovated the stands, etc. making the ballpark also useful for carnivals, concerts and festivals. He benefited financially owning the Dyckman Oval, as he didn't have to schedule games through booking agents, which cut into owners' profits.

Pompez made most of his money by being a "numbers man" (illegal lottery) in Harlem. He was eventually arrested for his involvement as was mobster Dutch Shultz. Pompez fled to Venezuela, but was captured but the authorities who would not extradite him to the United States. He became bored and, not making any money, he contacted the New York authorities in the person of Thomas Dewey and decided to return to the U.S. and testify against mobsters, only if he was forgiven for his involvement. Mr. Dewey agreed. After Pompez testified, he returned to baseball.

Upon returning to the United States, Pompez opened a liquor store in Harlem. He still remained a "numbers man," but was clever enough not to be arrested - or else he paid the authorities to turn their heads. Pompez was very generous toward the people residing in Harlem. He would buy food, pay rent and even loan (without payment) money to families for their children to attend Catholic area schools.

In 1924, Pompez negotiated the first Negro League World Series. The Champion team of the Negro National League (NNL) would play the Champion team of the Eastern Colored League (ECL).

Pompez became a scout for the New York Giants, and eventually became Director of International Scouting. He scouted many Latin players who eventually made it into the Major Leagues, including Orlando Cepeda, the Alou brothers and Jose Tartabull. There were reports that Pompez had his hand in the signing of Willie Mays for the New York Giants as well.

29

CUMBERLAND POSEY

BORN: CUMBERLAND WILLIS POSEY on June 20,
   1890 in Homestead, Pennsylvania
DIED: March 28, 1946 in Pittsburgh, Pennsylvania
NICKNAME: CUM
Inducted into the National Baseball Hall of Fame in
   2006

Cumberland "Cum" Posey, who attended both Penn State and Duquesne Universities, was the owner of the Homestead Grays. In his younger days, Cum was one of the top basketball players in the Pittsburgh area, which led him to play basketball at both Penn State and Duquesne. Using the organizational skills learned from basketball, Posey then became involved in baseball. In 1918 he became part-owner of the local Pittsburgh team, the Homestead Grays, with Charlie Walker, a local businessman.

The Grays were mainly a barnstorming team, playing throughout the Pennsylvania area. Posey was approached about having the Grays join the Eastern Colored League, but turned down the offer because they were making money barnstorming.

The Homestead Grays home base was Forbes Field, officially owned by the Pittsburgh Pirates of Major League Baseball's National League. The Grays were successful at home and on the road. By 1926, they were dominating opponents, posting a 140-13 record, and at one time winning 43 consecutive games.

They won 27 straight games in 1927. It was then Posey and Walker decided to have the Grays join the East-West League, which they dominated in the Pittsburgh area.

Posey began to argue with Gus Greenlee, owner of the Pittsburgh Crawfords, who was attempting to spearhead the new Negro National League. At the time the Grays began having financial difficulties in paying their players, such as stars Oscar Charleston, Josh Gibson and Judy Johnson. They all eventually left the Grays and were lured to the Crawfords by Greenlee, who promised them more money than they were being paid by Posey.

Finally, in 1934, Posey approached Rufus "Sonny" Jackson to help financially stabilize the Grays. Jackson was a local numbers man in the Homestead area. He also owned and leased jukeboxes to owners of local night clubs in the area. Posey and Jackson reached an agreement on running the Grays. Jackson would be the President and Treasurer, and Posey would run the everyday operations of the club.

The Grays then joined the Negro National League in 1934. But in 1935, Posey relinquished his managerial responsibilities to Vic Harris, who came from the Pittsburgh Crawfords. In 1937, Posey then became Secretary of the Negro National League.

The Homestead Grays then moved their home field to Griffith Stadium in Washington, D.C. They remained there through the

1948 season.

Eventually Josh Gibson was convinced to rejoin the Homestead Grays, and along with Buck Leonard, made the lineup stronger. The Homestead Grays became the leading dynasty in black baseball history.

Besides ownership of the Homestead Grays, Cum Posey worked for the Federal Postal Service at Penn (Railroad) Station located in Pittsburgh. He was also the Athletic Director of Homestead High School. Posey was also a member of the Homestead Board of Education from 1931 until his death in 1946. He sponsored local basketball, baseball, football, and boxing events.

He became a columnist for the *Pittsburgh Courier*, owned by his father. His column was called, "Pointed Paragraphs" from December 1931- April 1936 and "Posey Points" from May 1936 - June 1945.

When Posey died in 1946, he left his half of the Grays to his widow, but Jackson ran the club.

When the 1948 season ended, the Homestead Grays again became an independent baseball team. Jackson died in 1949, and the Grays eventually disbanded in 1951.

As a final fitting tribute, Cum Posey was inducted into the Basketball Hall of Fame in 2016.

30

LOUIS SANTOP

BORN: *LOUIS SANTOP LOFTIN on January 17, 1890 in Tyler, Texas*
DIED: *January 22, 1942 in Philadelphia, Pennsylvania*
Nickname: *"Top"*
Inducted into the Baseball Hall of Fame in 2006

Santop was a power-hitting catcher who often hit over .300 while playing in the Negro League. Many great athletes played Negro ball in the 1910's and 1920's, but Santop was one of the standouts in the Negro League. Rollo Wilson, a teammate of Santop on the Philadelphia Giants, once said, "If Rube Walker, the manager of the Giants, ever wrote about the history of baseball, he would no doubt list Santop as his first-string catcher."

Santop was well known for his powerful arm. On time, after a game, he stood at home plate and threw a ball over the centerfield fence, which was over 430 feet away.

In 1909 Santop, who for an unknown reason dropped his birth name of "Loftin," began his professional baseball career with the Fort Worth Wonders. This was the first time he was being paid to play baseball.

• • •

Before Santop retired in 1926, he had played for numerous teams in the Negro League, including the Oklahoma Monarchs, the Philadelphia Giants, the Lincoln Stars, the American Giants, the Brooklyn Royal Giants and the Hilldale Daisies.

The Lincoln Giants, one the strongest Negro clubs in the history of black baseball, was formed in 1911 by Jess McMahon, a white boxing promoter, along with his brother, Rod. The lineup included future Hall of Famers, "Smokey" Joe Williams and Cannonball Dick Redding, infielders Home Run Johnson and John Henry Lloyd, outfielder Spot Poles and catcher Louis Santop. These players were considered the greatest in the Negro League. They began playing in Olympic Field in Harlem, New York against semi-pro and Major League all-star teams several times a week. They drew crowds that often numbered in the thousands. At that time baseball was prohibited on Sundays in New York. The Lincoln Giants got around the ban by admitting fans free, then sold programs for 50 cents in the grandstands and 25 cents in the bleachers. Anyone refusing to pay for a program was immediately removed from the stadium.

The American Giants were managed in 1914 by future Hall of Famer Rube Foster. Besides Santop, Oscar Charleston was also on the team, bringing a total of five future Hall of Famers sharing the field together.

Santop enjoyed a lot of success and some notable achievements while playing for the Hilldale Daisies. In 1921, 1924 and 1925, the Daisies played in the Black World Series. They were victorious, and crowned the champions, in both 1921 and 1925. In 1924, when Hilldale played against white Major Leaguers, Santop batted .296.

· · ·

Santop enlisted in the United States Navy in 1918-19, but was immediately discharged after taking a medical examination. Ironically, the reason for his discharge was that a man with one of the most powerful arms in the Negro League was determined by the Navy to have a damaged, crooked arm!

The Hilldale team played an exhibition game in 1920 against the New York Yankees and Babe Ruth. Hilldale beat the Yankees. Santop had three hits in his four at bats, while Ruth went hitless. It has been said that Santop often went to bat, and "a la Babe Ruth," indicated he was going to hit a home run.

When Santop retired in 1926 he had compiled an impressive lifetime batting average of .406. After retiring, Santop stayed involved in baseball by becoming a broadcaster in Philadelphia.

Santop Lifetime stats

At Bats:	1209
Batting Average:	.406
Hits:	399
Home Runs:	16
Triples:	22
Doubles:	66
Runs Scored:	196
Runs Batted In:	210
Walks:	92
Stolen Bases:	34

31

MULE SUTTLES

BORN: George Suttles on March 31, 1901 at Blocton, Alabama
DIED: July 9, 1966 at Newark, New Jersey
NICKNAME: "Mule"
Inducted into the Baseball Hall of Fame in 2006

George "Mule" Suttles emerged from the Alabama coal mines to become one of the greatest power hitters in Negro League history. He was compared to Babe Ruth for his tape measured home runs, as well for his batting average. It is estimated Suttles had a batting average of .317.

He was popular and respected by the fans and players as well. When he came to bat the fans would cheer and chant, "Kick, Mule, Kick."

George was born about 40 miles southwest of Birmingham, Alabama. It was a coal mining boomtown. He worked in the mines as a teenager, and baseball was always his main diversion. The Suttles Family decided to move in 1920 to the Edgewater Coal Mining Camp, just 10 miles from Birmingham.

. . .

He briefly worked in the coal mines, but baseball was a burning desire. He left the coal mines in 1922 to play professional baseball with the Birmingham Black Barons. In his first game with the Barons, Suttles played left field and batted cleanup. He had a terrific game at bat with two singles, a double and a home run.

The following year, 1924, the Black Barons joined the Negro National League. Suttles continued his great playing both in the field and at bat. He was a fierce hitter, and he could throw with accuracy to any part of the field. His teammate, Dick Seay, said, "You could feel the earth quake when Suttles swung his bat and made contact with the ball."

Suttles left the Black Barons in 1926, joining the St. Louis Stars. In his first game, he slugged two home runs, including a grand slam, in the Stars rout 17-2 of the Cleveland Elites. The St. Louis Stars were considered one of the best teams in Negro league history.

After the 1929 season, Suttles decided to play Winter Ball in Cuba. In his first game, he hit a monster home run over 500 feet. The ball went out of the ballpark and landed in the ocean.

During most of the Negro League era, players bounced from team to team to make better wages. Suttles was no different. He left the St. Louis Stars in 1930 and joined the Detroit Wolves. He was traded in 1932 to the Washington Pilots. From 1933-1935 he played for the Chicago American Giants and was selected to play in the East-West All-Star Classic at Comiskey Park in Chicago. On August 11, playing in the All-Star Classic, he walked four times, struck out once, and saved the best for last.

Facing East pitcher Satchel Paige in the bottom of the 11th inning with two men on base and two out, Suttles drilled a home run over the right centerfield fence to give the West a thrilling 11-8 win. Sportswriter William G. Nunn wrote, "It was a mighty Kick of a Mighty Mule" a feat, "that fans in years to come will tell their children, grandchildren and their children's grandchildren about."

After the Classic, Suttles decided in 1936 to move on when he joined the Newark Eagles with whom he played until 1940.

In 1937, the *Pittsburgh Courier* called the Eagles infield, "The Dream Infield" while others called it "The Million Dollar Infield." By whatever name they were called, they were great. The infield consisted of Suttles at first base, Dick Seay at second base, Willie Wells at shortstop and Ray Dandridge at third base.

Mule Suttles decided to try his hand at managing. In 1943 he decided to manage the Newark Eagles. He became a mentor to both Monte Irvin and Larry Doby, who were teammates on the Eagles. Both eventually had great careers and were inducted into the Baseball Hall of Fame.

Suttles decided to retire in 1948. He remained in Newark, New Jersey and died at the age of 65 in 1966. Some of his former teammates were his pallbearers. He told them, "When I die, have a little thought for my memory, but don't mourn me too much."

<u>Suttles Lifetime Stats</u>:

At Bats:	2632
Batting Average:	.329
Hits:	866
Home Runs:	129
Triples:	73
Doubles:	257
Runs Scored:	540
Runs Batted In:	511
Walks:	245
Stolen Bases:	58

32

BEN TAYLOR

BORN: BENJAMIN HARRISON TAYLOR on July 1, 1888 in Anderson, South Carolina
DIED: January 24, 1953 in Baltimore, Maryland
NICKNAME: "Ben" & "Old Reliable"
Inducted into the Baseball Hall of Fame in 2006

Taylor was a first baseman. He began playing in the Negro League in 1908 until he retired in 1944. He played for numerous teams, including the American Giants, Birmingham Giants, Washington Potomacs, Harrisburg Giants, Baltimore Black Sox and Indianapolis ABC's. He played on the ABC's with his two brothers, Jim and Johnnie, from 1915-1922.

Taylor was a hard-hitting slugger, anchoring the ABC's lineup in the cleanup slot. There are recorded statistics of Ben Taylor's hitting prowess for the years 1920-1922. He hit for averages of .323, .407 and .358. Baseball historian James Riley said of Ben Taylor, "Modest, easygoing and soft-spoken. Taylor was a true gentleman who maintained a fair and professional demeanor, and he was an excellent teacher to the young players."

He originally began playing as a pitcher in 1908 when he played with the Birmingham Giants. Taylor was one of the best pitchers in the Negro League for two years. In 1909, his record was 22-3 and in 1910 it was 30-1.

Ben Taylor went to Cuba in 1915 and 1916 to play Winter Ball. He explained, "My reason for going to Cuba, after speaking with other black players, was that they were treated better and they made good money." Both years Taylor's batting average in Cuba was .500.

Taylor batted over .300 in fifteen of the first sixteen years of his career in the Negro League. His teammates applauded him, "Taylor is one of the best fielders and hitters in the Negro League."

In 1935, *The Chicago Defender* described Taylor as, "A man who inspired, trained and led teams for many years."

Biographer Todd Bolton noted, "Ben Taylor's life can be summed up from 10 words on his gravestone, "A graceful player, a superb teacher and a true gentleman."

Buck Leonard admitted, "I got most of my learning from Ben Taylor. He had to be the best first baseman in the Negro League. He was the one who really taught me how to play first base."

• • •

Ben Taylor belonged to one the most famous families in African-American baseball history. He had a 40-year career as a player and manager.

<u>Taylor's Lifetime Stats</u>:

Games:	300
At Bats:	2654
Batting Average:	.319
Hits:	845
Home Runs:	23
Triples:	56
Doubles:	142
Runs Scored:	380

33

CRISTOBAL TORRIENTE

BORN: *November 16, 1893 in Cienfuegos, Cuba*
DIED: *April 10, 1938 in New York City, New York*
NICKNAME: *"Carlos"*
Inducted into the National Baseball Hall of Fame in 2006

In 1914 Cristobal Torriente came from Cuba to play baseball in America. While here, over the course of his career he played for the Cuban Stars in the Negro League (1914-1915), All Nations in Western Independent League (1916-1917), the Chicago American Giants (1919-1925), the Kansas City Monarchs (1926) and the Detroit Stars (1927-1928) in the Negro National League, the Atlanta Crackers in the Independent Minor League and the Cleveland Cubs (1932) back in the Negro National League.

Torriente was a lefthanded power hitter. Although he could hit to all fields, Torriente was especially great hitting the ball to right field. He often hit the ball off the outfield fence. One such time offered evidence of how hard he hit the ball. Jelly Gardner, a teammate of Torriente on the American Giants, commented, "The New York Giants had a scout following our team to Kansas City, St Louis, and Indianapolis. The scout was watching Torriente who hit a line drive in Indianapolis that hit the top of the right-field wall and the right fielder threw him out at first base. That's how much power he had." Gardner further added, "The Giant scout liked Torriente and would have signed him, except for the fact he had kinky hair."

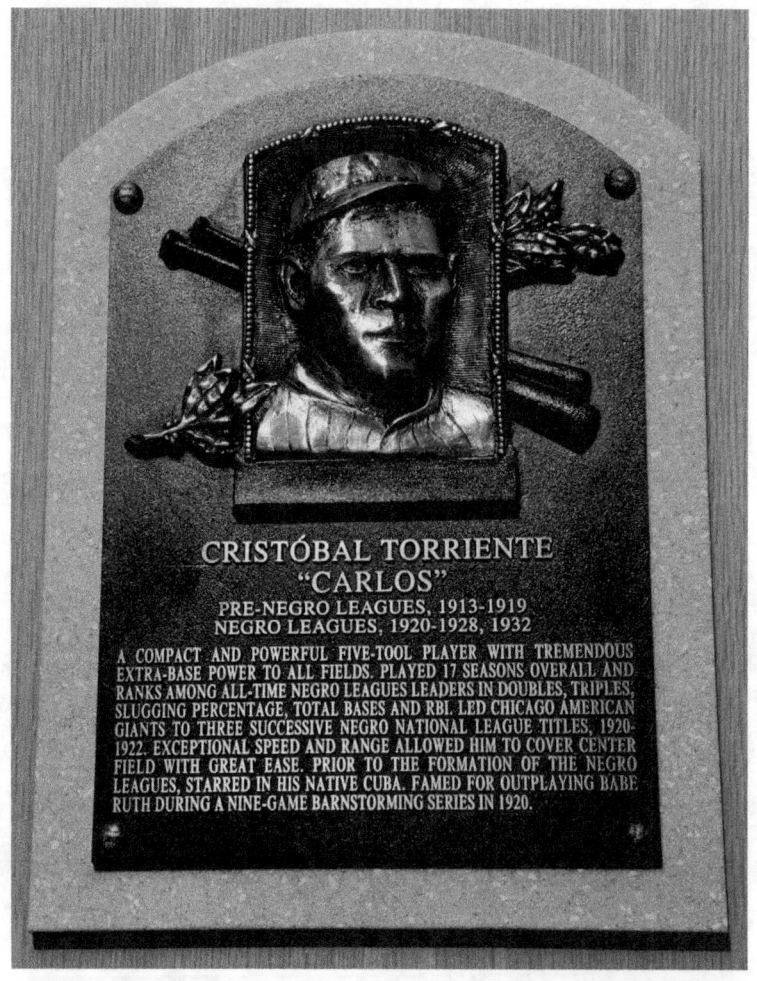

Torriente had an accurate arm, making him a good pitcher as well, enabling him to compile a 21-14 record in the Negro National League. He started close to 40 games and only gave up four home runs in his career. C.I. Taylor, the manager of the Indianapolis ABC's, once said, "If I should see Torriente walking across the street, I would say, 'There walks a ballclub.'"

The Chicago American Giants won three consecutive pennants in 1920, 1921 & 1922, the beginning of the Negro National League. In those years Torriente had batting averages of .402, .338, and .342. He won the batting title in 1920 and 1923, batting .402 each year.

In 1926 Torriente's batting average was .381 playing for the Kansas City Monarchs - which led the team.

Writer John Holway shared a few incidents of Torriente's life prior to playing baseball and during his baseball career. Holway remembered that Torriente, at 17 years old, joined the Cuban Army. He was placed in an Artillery Unit because of his husky build, which would enable him to lift the heavy artillery pieces.

On November 4, 1920, John McGraw brought the New York Giants to Cuba to play a series of games against the Almendures team, the team Torriente played on. Babe Ruth also came with the New York Giants. It was rumored that a huge sum of money was paid to Ruth in order to get him to join the Giants in Cuba.
During the third game between the Giants and Almendures, Torriente hit two monster home runs, driving in a total of four runs, beating the New York Giants and Babe Ruth 4-2. In this game, Ruth had a single and struck out twice.

• • •

In the next game, Babe Ruth took the mound to pitch. When Torriente came to bat the crowd began to cheer. Torriente smacked a hard line drive past Frankie Frisch, the third baseman, and Torriente wound up on second base driving in two runs. Holway noticed, "Ruth had a terrible frown on his face."

The Almendures beat the New York Giants, 11-4. Torriente finished both games with three home runs, one double and six RBI's. He outclassed Babe Ruth, who finished both games with only one single.

Torriente was noted for having a bad temper when he played baseball in Cuba. He was thrown out of one game after kicking at an umpire. Torriente refused to leave the team bench where he sat in street clothes. The umpire had him removed and escorted him to the bleachers by a police officer to watch the remainder of the game. On November 23, 1915, during another game, Torriente became furious when Umpire Kelly called him out attempting to steal third base. Torriente jumped up tossing dirt on the umpire. He was thrown out of the game.

Again in 1923, Torriente lost his temper in a game when Umpire Gholson, in Torriente's mind, made a bad call at second base. Torriente began to berate the umpire with awful language, then picked up dirt and threw it onto the umpire's trousers. He was ejected from the game.

Sadly, in 1938 Cristobal Torriente was living in New York City, suffering from alcoholism and ill from tuberculosis. He was found in his apartment by his good friend and fellow Hall of Fame inductee, Martin Dihigo. Dihigo, along with another friend, brought Torriente to the hospital, where he remained until he died on April 10, 1938. He is buried in Calvary Cemetery in Queens, New York.

Torriente's Lifetime Batting Stats:

At Bats:	2838
Batting Average:	.331
Hits:	953
Home Runs:	52
Triples:	67
Doubles:	177
Runs Batted In:	404
Walks:	339
Stolen Bases:	113

Pitching Statistics:

Games Started	38
Games Completed:	23
Innings Pitched:	339
Wins:	21
Losses:	14
Strikeouts:	134
Walks:	128
Home Runs Allowed:	4

34

SOLOMON WHITE

BORN: KING SOLOMON WHITE on June 12, 1868
   at Bellaire, Ohio
DIED: August 26, 1955 at Central Islip, New York
NICKNAME: "SOL"
Inducted into the Baseball Hall of Fame in 2006

*M*any of the Negro League inductees in the Baseball Hall of Fame owe a debt of gratitude to Sol White. He and Rube Foster are widely acclaimed to have kept black baseball afloat in the early part of the twentieth century. Their efforts eventually led to Jackie Robinson's debut into the Major League in 1947. John Holway refers to Sol White as, "An infielder who would go on to become the most influential figure in the first decade of Negro baseball." Today, White is often referred to as "Renaissance Man" due to his contributions in recording baseball history. He published a book entitled *History of Colored Base Ball*, also known as *Sol White's Official Base Ball Guide*. The book tells the story of early black players who entered the Negro League and the difficulties they experienced because of the color of their skin. The book also showcases the immense talents of many of those players. His writings provided a detailed source of early African-American baseball that would prove invaluable to later Negro baseball researchers. Many Northeastern newspapers neglected to report about the Negro player; that was the main reason why Sol White insisted on authoring his book—to make the public aware of the great black baseball players. In his book he describes the horrors these black players went through while playing in the South. He gives a detailed version of their schedules, the places where blacks played, their means of transportation, such as the beat-up old buses or cars in which these players traveled throughout the country in order to play the game they loved. Sol White further indicates how white players in the South refused to play with or against the black players.

White also addresses how these black players traveling down South were denied accommodations in many hotels owned by white proprietors.

Sol White goes so far as to name individuals who hated blacks, and therefore didn't want to see colored baseball players in the game at all. One of those was Adrian C. "Cap" Anson of the Chicago National League team. He showed complete disregard for the colored baseball player. He indicates how Anson was all for segregation in baseball. White concluded, "In no other profession has the color line been drawn more rigidly than in baseball." He further indicates the disparity in the salaries between major league players and colored players.

White's book became scarce to find because of the refusal to reprint it. There were only three known in existence, one each at the Baseball Hall of Fame Library, and the New York Public Library's African-American Culture Center, and one in the hands of a private collector. Upon White's insistence, and due to the interest in black baseball becoming popular, his book was reprinted twice in 1984.

His work and book still stand as the most researched and informed history of black baseball. It goes without saying Sol White and his resurrected book have kept the history of black baseball still alive and known today.

Sol White began his professional baseball career at 19 years of age with the Pittsburgh Keystones in 1887. The Keystones were part of the short-lived league called "The Colored Baseball Clubs."

Sol White was a terrific infielder, sought after by many teams. Back then, players moved often from team to team in order to make more money, and White was no exception. Between 1889 and 1907, Sol White bounced around with many teams such as New York Gothams, Cuban Giants, Page Fence Giants, Cuban X-Giants, Chicago Giants and Philadelphia Giants.

In 1901, Sol White entered into a partnership with two white sportswriters in Philadelphia, H. Walter Schlicter and Harry Smith, to form the Philadelphia Giants. White was the team's Player/Manager until 1909. In their inaugural season, the Philadelphia Giants season record was 81 wins, 43 loses and 2 ties.

Sol White approached Rube Foster in 1904, convincing Foster to join the Philadelphia Giants as their pitcher. Foster remained with the Philadelphia Giants from 1904-1906.

White decided to retire in 1911 as an active player but he didn't abandon baseball. Instead, he became Manager of the Boston Giants in 1912. In 1924 he then managed the Cleveland Browns in the Negro National League, later becoming manager of the Newark Stars in 1926. The Newark Stars were affiliated with the Eastern Colored League.

When Sol White decided to finally leave baseball, he worked as a journalist for the *New York Amsterdam News* and *The New York Age*.

Sol White is buried in Frederick Douglass Cemetery in Staten Island, New York. He had an unmarked grave for over three decades until 2012, when out of the goodness of the Negro

League Baseball Grave Marker Project, White finally had a gravestone placed at his gravesite. The stone, made of black granite, bears the following, "King Solomon (Sol) White." It depicts an etched photo of White.

J. LESLIE WILKINSON

BORN: JAMES LESLIE WILKINSON on May 14, 1878 in Alger, Iowa
DIED: August 21, 1964 in Kansas City, Missouri
NICKNAMES: "J.L." & "Wilkie"
Inducted into the National Baseball Hall of Fame in 2006

Wilkinson was the most respected and influential figure in the history of black baseball. In 1920, Wilkinson helped start the Negro National League. He was the founder and operator of the Kansas City Monarchs.

When Wilkinson was 17 years old, he played baseball using the pseudonym "Joe Green" to protect his amateur status so he could play college baseball. His desire to become a professional baseball player was dashed when he broke his wrist.

In 1904, with his wrist healed, Wilkinson joined Hopkins Brothers Sporting Goods, a semi-pro team. He played shortstop and eventually became the team captain. In 1907, Wilkinson booked their games at fairs, carnivals, festivals and reunions which drew crowds to benefit the team financially. In 1908, the team had a record of 31 wins and 2 losses.

Wilkinson founded a female team called, "Bloomer Girls." He had fun with the team, which also included three males. They had a bulldog for a mascot.

Wilkinson had another clever idea to promote baseball. He recruited Native Americans, African Americans, Chinese, Japanese, Hawaiians, Frenchmen, Cubans, Filipinos, Germans, Jews and White Americans onto a team called "All Nations." In 1913 the team traveled the country playing games from the East Coast to the West Coast. Their record that year was 119 wins and only 17 losses.

In 1918, Wilkinson entered the military during World War I. After his discharge, he returned and revived the All Nations team to include future Baseball Hall of Famers Jose Mendez and Cristobal Torriente.

1920, Wilkinson had the Kansas City Monarchs join the Negro National League. They were the best team during their first season. The Monarchs won the Negro National League four times (1923, 1924, 1926 and 1929) in that decade.

Both Jackie Robinson and Satchel Paige played for the Kansas City Monarchs after World War II. Wilkinson was responsible for Branch Rickey signing Robinson to the Montreal Monarchs in 1946.

During Wilkinson's reign, the Kansas City Monarchs boasted many players who were inducted into the National Baseball Hall of Fame, including "Cool Papa" Bell, Willard Brown, Andy Cooper, Bill Foster, Jose Mendez, Satchel Paige, Jackie Robinson, Bullet Joe Rogan, Hilton Smith, Turkey Stearnes and Willie Wells.

JUD WILSON

BORN: ERNEST JUDSON WILSON on February 28, 1894 in Remington, Virginia
DIED: June 27, 1963 in Washington, D.C.
Nicknames: "JUD" and "BOOJUM"
Inducted into the National Baseball Hall of Fame in 2006

*E*rnest Judson "Jud" Wilson was born in Remington, Virginia. There was much confusion as to his year of birth, which was listed as 1899. But eventually his birth year became 1894 after his wife Betty contacted the Hall of Fame. The year 1894 is engraved on his Hall of Fame plaque as well as his gravestone. To confuse matters further, the census records list 1897 as his year of birth. Wilson himself put it this way, "These fellows in our league lie too much about their ages."

Wilson entered the U.S. Army on June 29, 1918. He served in World War I as a corporal with Company D, 417th Service Battalion. When he was discharged from the Army he settled in

Washington, D.C. and played baseball with a semi-pro team in his Foggy Bottom neighborhood.

It was here where Jud was discovered by Scrappy Brown, shortstop of an independent Negro team, the Baltimore Black Sox. Brown encouraged Wilson to go to Baltimore and try out for the Sox, which he did, and joined the team after the tryout. Wilson lasted only two weeks before he left because he became disenchanted with Baltimore. Brown found Wilson and talked him into coming back to join the team. Wilson did, but again left the team. Again, Brown spoke with Wilson, who for a third time returned to Baltimore and played with the Sox.

This time Wilson stayed. It wasn't long before Wilson's teammate tagged him with the nickname, "Boojum," for his line drives that smashed against the outfield walls.

Wilson had a great season in 1925, batting .354, but the Black Sox were unable to overtake the Hilldale Club for the championship. On the Hilldale Club were future Hall of Famers Judy Johnson and Biz Mackey.

After the 1925 season, Wilson decided to play Winter Ball in Cuba. He arrived in Cuba and joined the Habana Leones of the Cuban Winter League. He led the team with a .430 batting average. He hit a rare home run over the rightfield fence in Almendare Park, a distance of over 400 feet. In doing so, he joined an elite group - Cristobal Torriente, Oscar Charleston, Alejandro Oms and Esteban Montalvo - as the only players to do so. Because of this, Wilson's teammates began calling him "El Jorocan" - "The Bull."

Jud Wilson is considered one of the best hitters in the Negro League. He played 24 years in the Negro League (1924-1945) for the Baltimore Black Sox, Homestead Grays, Pittsburgh Crawfords and Philadelphia Giants. In 16 seasons, Wilson batted over .300 and four times over .400.

Wilson played for the Homestead Grays at the age of 45, where he batted .468 in his first season.

Josh Gibson once said, "Wilson was the best hitter he ever saw." Ted Radcliffe, a Negro League player said about Wilson, "He was even a better hitter than Josh Gibson." Satchel Paige said, "Jud Wilson was one of the greatest hitters he ever faced."

Even though Wilson was recognized as a great player by his fans and teammates, he had a flaw in his personality. Many players were afraid of him, as he had a bad temper. He was considered one of the "Big Four of the Big Badmen" in the black baseball era. Clint Thomas feared, "He would kill you."

Prior to retiring, Wilson began displaying odd behavior and acting irrationally. Buck Leonard remembered, "During a game Wilson was making circles with his finger around third base. He would do the same thing with his bat when up at the plate." Another incident exhibiting Wilson's irrational behavior is told by another teammate, Jake Stephens. Stephen's said, "After the East-West All-Star Classic Jud went back to his room at the hotel. I went out with some of the players into the town and partied. I admit I got pretty inebriated. I returned to our hotel room and was somewhat boisterous which pissed off Wilson to no end as he was trying to sleep. When I proceeded being loud, Jud jumped up from his bed, grabbed me and tossed me toward the window in the room. He hung me out the window upside down. I must admit, I sobered up somewhat. Wilson finally brought me back into the room and pushed me down onto my bed, where I fell asleep. Lesson well learned."

. . .

Despite his odd behavior, Jud Wilson was an integral part of the teams he played on, some of which are considered the greatest in black baseball history.

<u>Jud Wilson' Lifetime Stats</u>:

At Bats:	3453
Batting Average:	.341
Hits:	1176
Home Runs:	79
Triples:	42
Doubles:	190
Runs Scored:	698
Runs Batted In:	404
Walks:	233
Stolen Bases:	97

37

JOHN WESLEY DONALDSON

BORN: JOHN WESLEY DONALDSON on February 20, 1891 in Glasgow, Missouri
DIED: April 14, 1970 in Chicago, Illinois

John Donaldson pitched during the Pre-Negro league and in Negro League baseball. His career apparently spanned over 30 years, as he played for numerous teams both in the semi-pro and Negro leagues. He played for All Nations, a team of mixed races, and the Monarchs. Both teams were owned by J.L. Wilkinson.

Apparently through extensive research, it was determined in his semi-pro and Negro League career that Donaldson pitched in 667 games with over 400 wins, 5,081 strikeouts and 14 no-hitters. He was considered by many to be the greatest pitcher of that era.

· · ·

During his early years, Donaldson played for the Missouri Black Tigers in 1908, and then for the Hannaca Blues, an all-black team from Glasgow.

Donaldson eventually joined a barnstorming team, the Tennessee Rats, owned by W.A. Brown of Holden, Missouri. They played all over the Midwest with a roster of about 20 players. They played during the day and their minstrel group played at night for mostly white ticket holders.

During his tenure with the Tennessee Rats, Donaldson was an excellent pitcher, posting a record of 44-3. He pitched an 18-inning game, striking out 31, and also had another 27-strikeout game.

On at least four separate occasions he struck out 19. In 1912, he moved on, playing for a team called the All Nations, which was based in Des Moines, Iowa. Donaldson's salary at the time was $150 a month. He pitched brilliantly for the team, which also included a woman using the pseudonym of Carrie Nation (like the temperance leader), and had players of mixed races. The All Nation team was successful traveling throughout the Midwest and Upper Midwest from 1912-1917.

During the 1915 season, Donaldson struck out on average 18 batters a game, and 31 in one 18-inning game.

Besides opponents and newspaper clippings, many fans all recollected that Donaldson struckout more than 500 batters that season, doing it three years straight. He accomplished this feat both playing for semi-pro and professional Negro league teams.

· · ·

Prior to the inaugural season of the Negro National League in 1920, Donaldson's team played ball around the clock, traveling throughout the Midwest and as far west as Los Angeles, and as far east as Palm Beach, Florida.

The owner of All Nations, J.L. Wilkinson, was interviewed in 1948 by the *Kansas City Call* a local newspaper, where he bragged, "Donaldson is one of the greatest pitchers who ever lived, white or black." Wilkinson further noted, "Donaldson suggested the name Monarchs" as Wilkinson was preparing the team to enter the Negro National League in 1920.

When the Monarchs began playing in 1920, Donaldson was already 20 years of age and he began to play the outfield when not pitching. Wilkinson asked Donaldson to be the player/manager of the Monarchs, but he refused. That opened the door for Jose Mendez to become the player/manager of the Monarchs.

During this period, the Negro National League permitted players to play for other teams in order to make extra money. Donaldson barnstormed with a semi-pro team. It was also at this time he rejoined the All Nations team for two years as their player/manager. The team was also owned by J.L. Wilkinson. As player/manager, Donaldson instructed the younger players to sharpen their playing skills at bat as well as in the field. This prepared these players to move up to the "parent club," the Monarchs.

· · ·

When Donaldson barnstormed at this time, there was racial strife throughout the South at the instigation of the Klu Klux Klan. He was playing just three years after three black circus workers were lynched in 1920 in Duluth, Minnesota. He was the only black player on this team. He eventually pitched and beat an all-white All-Star team 6-3.

Baseball historian Pete Gorton believed, "Donaldson's character, composure and charisma were counter measures to the deep prejudices that existed at the time." He continued, "I don't think anyone believed white owners, players or fans exploited him. He was a man adored by everyone wherever he played."

Further proof of Donaldson's fame and fan appreciation came when the Editor of the newspaper in Melrose, Minnesota received a letter from a fan indicating, "Two-thirds of the attendance at Melrose games wanted to see Donaldson play. He was great and appreciated by all. We didn't mind seeing the Melrose or Scobey teams. We were more interested to see Donaldson play, whether on the mound or in the outfield."

After more than 30 years as a player, Donaldson retired in 1941. He settled in Chicago where it is believed he was employed with the U.S. Postal Service.

Although he himself never made it to the Major Leagues, he did become a full-time Coach for the Chicago White Sox from 1949-1950. He pursued Willie Mays and Ernie Banks, but Mays was signed by the New York Giants and Banks by the Chicago Cubs.

• • •

During this tenure as coach with the White Sox, Donaldson is credited with signing several Negro Leaguers at the time, such as Bob Boyd and Sam Hairston.

It is the opinion of this writer, that Donaldson should have been inducted into the Baseball Hall of Fame long ago, and definitely in 2006 when 35 Negro players and executives were inducted. He definitely had the credentials and character traits while playing. Let's hope he is inducted when the next Negro League players are inducted, whenever that takes place. As I have stated before, "Another forgotten hero in the Negro League - Buck O'Neil - should also be in the Hall of Fame."

38

BUCK O'NEIL

BORN: November 13, 1911 in Carrabelle, Florida
DIED: October 6, 2006 in Kansas City, Missouri
NICKNAMES IN HIS YOUTH: Jay, J.J. & Foot
NICKNAME AS ADULT: Buck & Country

In his youth, Buck O'Neil worked in a celery field where his father was the foreman. He would hand out boxes, which were then loaded with celery. One day it was exceptionally hot, and as Buck sat beside the celery boxes he commented, "Damn, there's got to be something better than this." Later that evening, his Dad told Buck he heard what he had said in the celery field. Buck thought for certain his Dad was going to punish him, but instead his Dad said to Buck, "To find something better, you will have to move away."

Buck received a scholarship to Edward Waters College, a black college in Jacksonville, Florida. The baseball coach, Ox Clemons, introduced himself to Buck and soon nicknamed him,

"Country." The coach made Buck a lineman on the football team besides having Buck play on the baseball team.

Upon graduation from College, Buck received a diploma as well as two years of college credit.

Soon after graduation Buck decided to play baseball for a semi-pro team, the Tampa Black Smokers in 1933. In 1934, he then was signed by Buck O'Neal (note the different spelling), the owner of the Miami Giants. Both teams were unofficial minor league clubs of the Negro League. Buck was paid $10 per week plus room and board with the barnstorming team.

Buck O'Neil then heard of a team called the New York Tigers who he tried out for and made the team. As Buck would say, "We had no affiliation with Harlem, New York, but the fans thought so." While the team barnstormed all over the West in two beat up Cadillacs, O'Neil, being adept in shooting pool, would win billiard competitions which would go toward feeding the team.

Soon Buck O'Neil decided to leave the Tigers and join a minor league team in 1936 which was affiliated with the Kansas City Monarchs. O'Neil finally made the parent team in 1939-1942. The Monarchs in 1942 won four straight Negro League pennants. O'Neil said, "The 1942 team was the greatest. Honestly, I think we could have beaten the New York Yankees."

O'Neil was eventually selected to play in the East-West All-Star Game. The Monarchs swept the Homestead Grays in the Negro League World Series.

· · ·

One Easter Sunday, in 1943, O'Neil hit for the cycle against Memphis. He recalled, "Although that was memorable, my most memorable incident that day was when I met my future wife, Ora Lee Owens." Their relationship was short-lived, as O'Neil was drafted into the U.S. Navy and was stationed in the Philippines. His unit was assigned to loading and off-loading equipment. O'Neil remembered, "We were treated badly as if we were still in the Jim Crow South." He further reflected, "I honestly believe if we ever captured a Jap, he would be treated better than us."

One day, while stationed in the Philippines, O'Neil's Commanding Officer informed O'Neil that the Dodgers had just signed Jackie Robinson to a contract and he would be playing for Montreal next year. O'Neil found the intercom and announced this over the entire ship. He recalled, "There was more noise because of this announcement than on VJ Day." He went on to say, "Integration was about to become a way of life - finally."

Upon being discharged from the Navy on January 17, 1946, O'Neil returned home and soon married Ms. Owens. He also returned to playing baseball with the Kansas City Monarchs. At the time they were playing the Newark Eagles, who eventually beat the Monarchs to win the World Series.

Soon after the loss, J.T Wilkinson sold the Monarchs to his partner, Tom Baird. Baird then named Buck O'Neil as the team's player/manager.

· · ·

At the end of the 1955 season, O'Neil decided to retire from the Kansas City Monarchs. He understood, "Statistics were very sketchy in the Negro Leagues. it was reported by *Baseball Reference* my batting average was .283; *Seamheads* had my lifetime batting average as .261 and the Center for Negro League Research listed my average as .303. Honestly, I don't doubt I had a .300 or better batting average."

After the 1955 season, Buck became a scout for the Chicago Cubs of the Major Leagues. One day he heard about a player who was a tremendous hitter and fielder. So, he rode on the backroads in Alabama, eventually arriving at the baseball field. He watched this player hit and field just as he was told. He immediately told the player, Oscar Gamble, he would sign him to a contract. Gamble went on to have a very successful 17-year career, especially a post career with the New York Yankees.

Buck O'Neil remained a scout with the Cubs on and off until 1988 when the Cubs made him the first black coach in Major League Baseball.

It should be noted, Buck O'Neil signed 13 eventual Major League players, such as Oscar Gamble, Lou Brock, Ernie Banks, Joe Carter and Lee Smith, to mention a few.

Buck O'Neil had a long desire to create a Negro Baseball Museum in Kansas City. It finally came to fruition in 1990 in conjunction with a friend, Frank Smith. They both paid the rent for space in a building, but then realized it was too small a space to place all the memorabilia. O'Neil bemoaned, "We need a complete building to display our memorabilia or else black baseball and those deserving players and their stories will never be told. It will die."

With the intervention of film director, Ken Burn's epic documentary, "Baseball," it enabled Buck O'Neil's dream of a permanent home for the Negro Baseball Museum to become a reality when it opened on November 11, 1997.

O'Neil soon began to rub elbows with the likes of Cab Callaway, Billie Holiday, Bojangles Robinson and even boxer Joe Louis, who all contributed their time and money to see the Museum remain afloat.

On Buck O'Neil's 94th birthday, he went to Washington, D.C. and asked and received permission from Congress to rename the Museum as the America Negro Baseball Museum.

As of this article, Buck O'Neil has not been inducted into the National Baseball Hall of Fame. Although there is a statue of him inside the Hall of Fame, the writer of this article wonders how he wasn't selected in 2006 along with the other Negro Inductees. He certainly deserved to be amongst them.

It also should be noted that, unlike so many inductees from the Negro League, Buck O'Neil played his entire eleven year career with one team, the Kansas City Monarchs.

<u>O'Neil's Lifetime Stats</u>:

At Bats:	782
Batting Average:	.283
Hits:	204
Triples:	12
Doubles:	17
Runs Batted In:	99
Walks:	36
Stolen Bases:	30

39

ROD CAREW

BORN: *Rodney Cline Carew on October 1, 1945 in
   Gatun, Panama, near the
Panama Canal
Inducted into the National Baseball Hall of Fame
   in 1991*

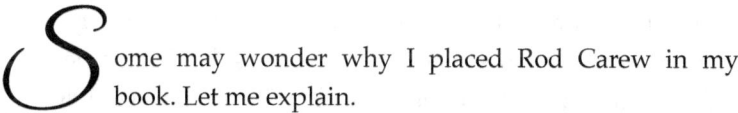ome may wonder why I placed Rod Carew in my book. Let me explain.

Growing up in Panama, Carew, his mother and brother experienced both physical and verbal abuse from his Dad. Ironically, he also experienced abuse while playing baseball with his peers in Panama.

Eventually Rod immigrated to the United States with his mother and brother. Carew was signed by the Minnesota Twins and sent to the minor leagues. He was verbally abused by teammates because they thought he was to cocky, rude and brash. He states his behavior no doubt is attributed to his experiences of abuse by his Dad while growing up in Panama.

Rod Carew like the thirty-five black ballplayers, was also inducted in the Baseball Hall of Fame. He was inducted in 1991. He was one of the greatest hitters ever to play in the Major League.

Interesting to say the least, Carew's mom, Olga, was traveling on a train to the hospital to give birth to Carew. It soon became apparent to her that she was not going to make it to the hospital as she began to experience contractions and began to deliver the baby. Olga was in luck, because on the train was a nurse, Margaret Allen, and a doctor, Dr. Cline, who delivered the baby, Rodney Cline Carew. Olga Carew gave Rod the middle name Cline after the doctor.

Further appreciation was shown by Olga in naming Margaret Allen, the nurse who assisted in the birth, as the Godmother. Ms. Allen was a true Godmother, as she later assisted Olga in preparing paperwork for her to leave Panama with Rod. The reason for this emigration to the United States was Carew's father, Erik, who was an alcoholic and abusive toward Olga, Rod and Rod's brother, Dickie. Olga's brother, Clyde Scott, gave financial assistance to them so they could leave Panama and move to New York City. Besides his brother, Dickie, Rod had three sisters.

Prior to leaving Panama, Rod Carew attended grade school where his gym teacher, Joseph French (brother-in-law of Olga), provided guidance to Rod.

• • •

Arriving in New York City, Rod Carew attended George Washington High School. At the time, Rod didn't speak English. He was a good baseball player but chose not to play baseball at George Washington High School. Instead he worked in a grocery store and studied his subjects and learned English.

It wasn't until 1964 that Rod Carew began playing baseball with a team called the Cavaliers in the Bronx Federation League. He was a great ball player, playing second base. He was also a fantastic hitter. He soon began playing baseball in the Spanish/Puerto Rican League in Central Park. Soon, Herb Stein, a New York City Transit Police Officer and part-time scout of the Minnesota Twins, noticed Carew, He observed, "He had strong wrists and, being he was a left-handed batter, he hit the ball with ease to left field." Herb Stein convinced the Minnesota Twins to sign Rod Carew.

Prior to reporting to his minor league team in Florida, Carew enlisted in the Marine Corps to fulfill his military obligation. Upon being discharged, he remained in the Reserves for four more years.

Rod Carew was assigned to a minor league team for the Minnesota Twins in the Florida State League in 1965. He played for the team for two years. In his first year, Carew batted .303 and stole 52 bases.

Carew was promoted to the parent club in 1967. He made his debut on April 11, 1967 and wasted no time showing and proving his hitting prowess. Against Dave McNally, Carew, in his first at bat, hit a single. He would finish getting two hits out of four at bats.

Much success awaited Carew in his first season with the Twins. He went on to bat .292 and was voted A.L. Rookie of the Year by the Baseball Writers Association and *Sporting News*.

His success continued; he was selected to play on the A.L. All-Star Team as the starting second baseman in 1967. Carew went on to play in eighteen (18) All-Star games in his career.

Rod Carew was considered one of the greatest hitters in the major leagues. Proof of his hitting prowess began in 1969, which was the first of seven seasons when he hit .300 or better. He led the American League in batting in 1972 (.318), 1973 (.350), 1974 (.364), 1975 (.359), 1977 (.388) and 1978 (.333). Carew's 1977 batting average of .388 was his highest, and for many years the highest in both leagues. Today, the Batting Title in the American League is named after Rod Carew.

For Rod Carew's hitting prowess, he was placed on the cover of *Sports Illustrated* and *The New York Times* on July 18, 1977.

During his career playing for the Minnesota Twins, Carew stole home seven times. Carew believed, "It is best to attempt to steal home early in the game as the opposing team most often is caught off guard."

Rod Carew was also the first Twins player to hit for what is called the cycle: a single, double, triple and home run. It doesn't matter what order this is done.

Rod Carew and Marilyn Levy were married on October 24, 1970. They have three daughters, Charryse, Stephanie and Michelle, but unfortunately, Michelle contracted leukemia and passed away. Rod and Marilyn divorced, and in 2015 Rod married Rhonda Jones. There is no listing of any children from this marriage.

Rod Carew and Ira Berkow teamed up to write his autobiography entitled *Carew*. It can be purchased on Amazon and Barnes and Noble.

Rod Carew was inducted into the National Baseball Hall of Fame in 1991, in his first year of eligibility. He was the first Panamanian to be inducted. The next one to receive this honor was Mariano Rivera of the New York Yankees. In 1977, Baseball decided to award Carew the Roberto Clemente Award, for his baseball career as well as his community service with the youth.

Rod Carew retired from baseball in 1985, and shortly thereafter the Minnesota Twins and California Angels, the two teams he played for, both retired his number 29. He is also in both teams' Halls of Fame. Carew was also inducted into the Caribbean Baseball Hall of Fame.

Rod Carew had fantastic statistics in his baseball career, his statistics were: .325 BA, 3,053 Hits, 445 Doubles, 112 Triples, 1,424 Runs scored, 353 Stolen bases, 92 homeruns and 1,015 RBI's.

• • •

After his playing career, Carew became a coach for the California Angels (1992-1999) and the Milwaukee Brewers (2000-2001).

During his career, Carew began chewing tobacco which eventually caused him jaw and dental problems. He spent a considerable amount of money on dental restoration.

In 2015, he suffered a massive heart attack, which required a ventricular replacement. He recovered nicely, but then his doctors informed him he would need a heart transplant, which was done on December 15, 2016. He received his heart from Konrad Reuland, a former NFL Baltimore Ravens tight end. Reuland was familiar with Carew as Reuland attended middle school with Rod Carew's children. In 2016, he was also awarded the Bob Feller Act of Valor.

Many people often wonder if Rod Carew ever won a World Series with the teams (Twins & Angels) he played for. He made it four times into the ALCS, twice with the Twins and twice with the Angels- but no never played in a World Series. Every baseball player dreams of winning a World Series.

Carew's Stats:

Batting Average:	.325
Hits:	3053
Home Runs:	92
Triples:	112
Doubles:	445
Runs Scored:	1424
Runs Batted In:	1015
Stolen Bases:	353

40

MILITARY HEROES OF THE NEGRO LEAGUES

*A*s a veteran of Vietnam and Desert Storm, it is my honor and privilege to write about the Heroes of the Negro League Hall of Famers who were in the military during World War I.

Along with the Negro League players who were in the military during World War I, there were other players who served in the military in World War II and Korean War who are also Hall of Famers. Just to mention a few, they are: Monte Irvin, Willard Brown, Leon Day, Ted Williams, Yogi Berra, Bob Feller, Stan Musial and Hank Greenberg.

The players and Hall of Famers who served in the military during the Korean War are: Ernie Banks, Willie Mays, Whitey Herzog, Eddie Mathews, Whitey Ford and Ted Williams, who served in World War II as well.

These four men, Oscar Charleston, Bullet Joe Rogan, Louis Santop and Jud Wilson played in the Negro League in the early 1900's. While playing baseball, they were drafted or joined the military at the start of World War I.

∙ ∙ ∙

I recently received an email from the Baseball Hall of Fame, honoring these men who entered the military to defend our freedom. These men left home, and soon found out that racial prejudice and segregation existed in the military just as at home. These men learned to deal with this problem just as they did while playing baseball in the States.

By the time segregation ended in baseball with the signing of Jackie Robinson in 1947, these men were deceased. No doubt these four men and other black players dealt with racial problems playing in the Negro League, but they would have played baseball in the Major League had they been alive.

Oscar Charleston first entered the Army at the age of 15. He lied about the year of his birth but the military authorities took his word. He was assigned to a unit in the Philippines, playing baseball on the same team as Bullet Rogan.

Rogan was discharged from the Army in 1914 but chose soon after to re-enlist, this time being assigned to the 25th Infantry. He was sent to join his unit in Hawaii, stationed at Schofield Barracks. He played baseball on the 25th Infantry team. In a short period of time, Rogan was transferred back to the States, going to Fort Stephen Little in Arizona.

While at Fort Stephen Little, Rogan joined the baseball team of the 25th Infantry Wreckers. Rogan played on the Wreckers from 1914-1918, when they were considered the best baseball team in that era.

∙ ∙ ∙

The owner of the Kansas City Monarchs, Hall of Famer J.L. Wilkinson, scouted members of the Wreckers, as well as Casey Stengel. Yes, the Casey Stengel who later became manager of the New York Yankees.

Wilkinson recruited a number of players on the Wreckers, including Rogan. These men originally were a barnstorming team called, "All Nations," which Wilkinson re-named the Kansas City Monarchs.

Jud Wilson joined the Army in June 1918. He served with Company D, the 417th Service Battalion, as a Corporal. Upon his discharge, he returned to the States and joined a semi-pro team, but soon was scouted and signed to play on the Baltimore Black Sox. Jud Wilson was a great home run hitter as well as an excellent fielder while playing in the Negro League for decades. He eventually joined the Homestead Grays. Wilson decided to play Winter Ball in Cuba, because the money was good and the living conditions much better than in the States. He said, "There was no racial discrimination, we were treated well by the fans, owners and players on the team."

Louis Santop was an early superstar playing baseball. He was a gifted home run hitter, earning the nickname "Big Bertha" from his teammates on the Army team. He was assigned to Fort Dix, New Jersey playing baseball on the same team with Cannonball Redding. Santop was discharged from the Army when he failed a physical where the Medical Staff discovered he had a twisted and broken arm. Therefore, he was classified as "Physically Unfit." He returned home, but soon decided to try and join the Navy. He took his entry physical and was found fit for duty.

• • •

He was assigned to a unit in Norfolk, Virginia where he remained playing baseball until he was discharged in 1919. At the time of his discharge, Santop was 29 years of age.

41

PHOTO GALLERY

12 Man Ball team

AC Jacket & Gloves Showcase

The Cuban Giants

Barnstorming on the Open Road

Barnstorming Teams

Birdwell Park Poster

Campanella, Doby, Newcombe & Robinson Photo

Chicago & St Louis Jerseys

Cleveland & KC Jersey Showcase

Dandridge, Barnhill & Willie Mays Photo

Double Day Field & Stands #2

Double Day Field with American Flag & Statue

Entrance to Double Day Field

It was not until 1959, when Pumpsie Green played for the Boston Red Sox, that every MLB team had integrated. But acceptance and inclusion in every aspect of the game remained an issue. In 1966, Emmett Ashford became the first black umpire for a major league game and in 1975 Frank Robinson finally broke the manager's color line, piloting the Cleveland Indians for three years.

Frank Robinson holding a 1971 newspaper, four years before he became manager of the Cleveland Indians.

Frank Robinson Photo with Daily News

Frank Robinson Showcase #3

Hall of Fame & Main St.

Hall of Fame Outside Photo

Hall of Fame #4

Hilldale Belt Buckle

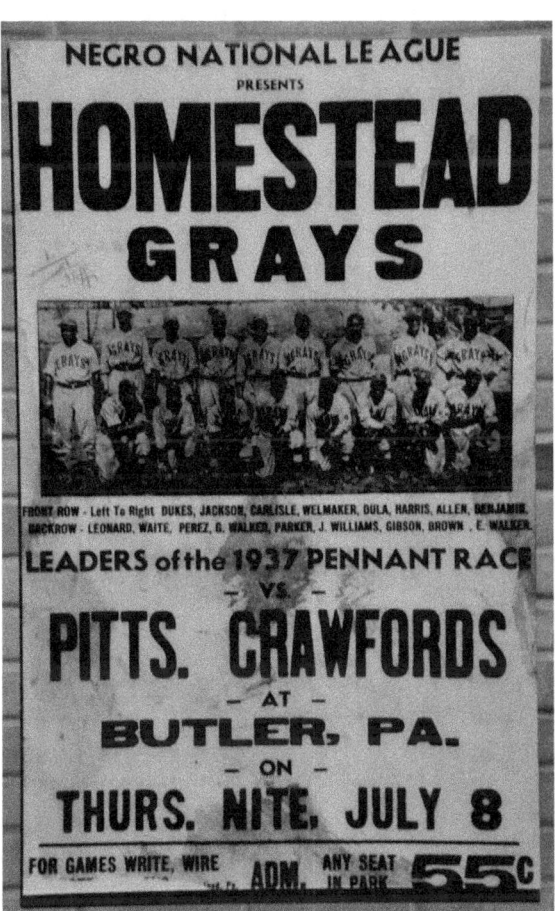

Homestead Grays Poster

Homestead Room with Memorabilia in Cases

Robinson served in the Army during World War II. Like many African Americans, he felt it was a war to end prejudice as well as a war for democracy. Though black soldiers served in segregated units until after the war, many were highly decorated. Their example helped highlight their right to full participation as citizens when peace came in 1945. Having served made Robinson somewhat older than the usual baseball recruit; but it was an important part of his past for Rickey and baseball fans.

Jackie Robinson in Military Uniform

Jackie Robinson Sliding to Home Plate

Man & Woman sitting down

Mexico Jersey Showcase

Negro National League Baseball 1942 Photo

Paige & Doby in Photo

Plaque room with lady

Plaque room with man

POST-INTEGRATION ERA
1959–Present

By 1959, every major league team's roster was integrated, but in baseball, as in all parts of American life, questions concerning true equality of opportunity remained unresolved. The presence of black players, managers or team officials was not always fully accepted or welcomed. Despite progress on many fronts in baseball, such issues continue to be discussed today.

Post Segregation ERA

Pride & Passion

Branch Rickey and Jackie Robinson

Branch Rickey assigned Dodgers scout Clyde Sukeforth to find an African-American player with major league talent and the courage to withstand harsh prejudicial treatment. Sukeforth found his man in Kansas City Monarchs shortstop Jackie Robinson. Despite opposition from major league owners, Rickey signed Robinson for the 1946 season.

Robinson & Rickey

Sand Lot Boy#2

SEPARATE LEAGUES, PARALLEL LIVES
1920-1932

The first of the Negro leagues, the Negro National League, was formed in 1920 by black owner-managers Rube Foster of the Chicago American Giants and C.I. Taylor of the Indianapolis ABCs. They hoped to lessen the effects of discriminatory practices of white-run booking agencies and to enhance opportunities for black players. A second league, the Eastern Colored League, formed for the 1923 season. These leagues prospered in the boom years of the 1920s, as many southern rural African Americans migrated to northern and Midwestern industrial cities.

Separate Lives Parallel Lives Poster

SIGNPOSTS FOR OPPORTUNITY
1947-1959

As World War II ended, many African Americans believed that "separate but equal" could no longer be tolerated because while much was separate, little was equal. Highly decorated black regiments helped foster the pride and impetus that demanded change in all parts of American life.

Following the death of commissioner Kenesaw Mountain Landis, Brooklyn Dodgers president Branch Rickey and Jackie Robinson took the lead in testing America's tolerance for integrated baseball. Under pressure, the major and minor leagues began to desegregate, but slowly and on their own terms.

Signposts for Opportunity Poster

Lou Gehrig, Jackie Robinson and Roberto Clemente

ACKNOWLEDGMENTS

This book would have been difficult to write without the support of my family. First, my heartfelt thanks to my wife Marie, for her support, encouragement, suggestions and help.

To my daughter Erica, for her cheerful ways each day, by encouraging me, then driving with me to the Baseball Hall of Fame in Cooperstown in order to take photos of the plaques of the Negro players who were inducted into the Hall, and other photos she helped me take. Many thanks to my daughter Michelle and son-in-law Owen for their computer expertise, helping me "surf" the internet as well as correcting my mistakes with formatting. A special thanks to my grandchildren, Jack and Dakota. They actually thought up the title of this book, *Heroes of the Baseball Negro Leagues*.

The book would never have been authored without the expertise, knowledge, help and guidance of my good friend, Jay Price. It was no mistake I asked for his help. Jay is a former sports columnist of a local newspaper, *Staten Island Advance*, and he is the author of a book entitled *Thanksgiving 1959*.

Thanks is extended to my friend and one-time co-worker Mario Mattei for his many hours of editing the manuscript of the book. To Jay and Mario, your time and effort in seeing this "rookie" author through his first book is most appreciated.

Thanks also to my partner in the NYPD, Cormac Gordon, who also is a former sports columnist in the *Staten Island Advance*. He suggested I contact Joe D'Amodio and Jerry Lee, both sports journalists there as well.

To Joe D'Amodio and Jerry Lee, thanks for listening to me, then offering your help in writing the article on Julie Bowers, Sonny Logan and Glenn Mosley - and also the surprise article on me.

Mark Washington, I thank you for providing me with the contact information to Gerry Mosley. Mark said, "Dan, ask Gerry for Willie Bowers and Betty Logan's phone numbers. They are all cousins, so he should have their numbers." Speaking with Gerry Mosley led me also to speak with Bowers and Logan.

As I previously indicated, thanks to my grandchildren for the title of this book, *Deferred Glory: Heroes of the Negro Baseball Leagues*. Hope you enjoy the book.

ABOUT THE AUTHOR

Born and bred in New York City, Danny Ingellis is a former Detective in the District Attorney's Squad and a lifelong seeker of the story behind the story.

His fascination with people and their stories has been a hallmark of his career, along with his mission to protect and preserve the values he lives every day. Ingellis has always gone above and beyond, whether as a combat veteran of both the Vietnam War and Operation Desert Storm, or in his professional career—when Ingellis became the personal bodyguard to

Richmond County District Attorney William Murphy, he donated his own kidney to save Murphy's life.

Once Ingellis retired, he pursued his passion for photography, and continued capturing stories from behind the lens. His freelance photos have appeared in many newspapers and books, and led him to sportswriter Andy Mele, who asked Ingellis to help with research for a book he intended to write on the thirty-five Negro Leaguers inducted into the National Baseball Hall of Fame.

When Mele unexpectedly passed away, Ingellis went above and beyond once more as he set out to fulfill his friend's dream and complete this book on the inductees whose stories need to be shared, now more than ever.

Ingellis lives on Staten Island and recently celebrated his fiftieth anniversary with his beautiful wife Marie. They have two beloved children, Michelle and Erica, and are the proud grandparents of Jack and Dakota.

www.ingramcontent.com/pod-product-compliance
Lightning Source LLC
Chambersburg PA
CBHW071232080526
44587CB00013BA/1576